Sleep Walking and Moon Walking

by Isidor Isaak Sadger

CONTENTS

Translator's Preface

Introduction

PART I. Medical

PART II. Literary Section

Conclusion

TRANSLATOR'S PREFACE

Psychoanalysis holds a key to the problem of sleep walking, which alone has been able to unlock the mysteries of its causes and its significance. This key is the principle of wish fulfilment, an interpretative principle which explains the mechanisms of the psyche and illuminates the mental content which underlies these. Sleep walking as a method of wish fulfilment evidently lies close to the dream life, which has become known through psychoanalysis. Most of us when we dream, according to the words of Protagoras, "lie still, and do not stir." In some persons there is however a special tendency to motor activity, in itself a symptomatic manifestation, which necessitates the carrying out of the dream wish through walking in the sleep. The existence of this fact, together with the evidence of an influence of the shining of the moon upon this tendency to sleep walking, give rise to certain questions of importance to medical psychology. The author of this book has pursued these questions in relation to cases which have come to him for psychoanalysis, in the investigation of actual records of sleep walking given in literature and in the study of rare instances where it has been made the subject of a literary production or at least an episode in tale or drama. In each case the association with moonlight or some other light has been a distinct feature.

The author's application of psychoanalysis to these problems has the directness and explicitness which we are accustomed to find in Freud's own writings. This is as true in the literary portion of the work as in the medical but it never intrudes to mar the intrinsic beauty of certain of the selections nor the force of the intuitive revelations which the writers of the preceding science have made in regard to sleep walking and walking in the moonlight. Sadger has skilfully utilized these revelations to convince us of the truth of the psychoanalytic discoveries and has used the latter only to make still more explicitly and scientifically clear the testimony of the poetic writers and to point out the applicability of their material to medical problems. The choice of this little understood and little studied subject and its skilful presentation on the part of the author, as well as the introduction to the reader of the literary productions of which use has been made, give the book a peculiar interest and value. It is also of especial service in its brief but profoundly suggestive study of the psychic background of Shakespeare's creative work as illustrated in the sleep walking of Lady Macbeth. The endeavor in the translation has been to make accessible to our English readers the clear and direct psychoanalysis of the author and the peculiar psychologic and literary value of the book.

INTRODUCTION[1]

[1] Nachtwandeln und Mondsucht. Eine medizinisch-literarische Studie, von Dr. J. Sadger, Nervenarzt in Wien; Schriften zur angewandten Seelenkunde, Herausgegeben von Prof. Dr. Sigm. Freud, Sechzehntes Heft, Leipzig und Wien, Franz Deuticke, 1914.

Sleep walking or night wandering, known also by its Latin name of noctambulism, is a well-known phenomenon. Somnambulism is not so good a term for it, since that signifies too many things. In sleep walking a person rises from his bed in the night, apparently asleep, walks around with closed or half opened eyes, but without perceiving anything, yet performs all sorts of apparently purposeful and often quite complicated actions and gives correct answers to questions, without afterward the least knowledge of what he has said or done. If this all happens at the very time and under the influence of the full moon, it is spoken of as moon walking or being moonstruck.

Under the influence of this heavenly body the moonstruck individual is actually enticed from his bed, often gazes fixedly at the moon, stands at the window or climbs out of it, "with the surefootedness of the sleep walker," climbs up upon the roof and walks about there or, without stumbling, goes into the open. In short, he carries out all sorts of complex actions. Only it would be dangerous to call the wanderer by name, for then he would not only waken where he was, but he would collapse frequently and fall headlong with fright if he found himself on a height.

Besides there is absolute amnesia succeeding this. Upon persistent questioning there is an attempt to fill in the gaps in memory by confabulation, like the effort to explain posthypnotic action. Furthermore, it is asserted that a specially deep sleep always ushers in night wandering, that indeed the latter in general is only possible in this condition. It is more frequent with children up to puberty and throughout that period than with adults. At the same time the first outbreak of sleep walking occurs often at the first appearance of sexual maturity. According to a widespread folk belief sleep walking will cease in a girl when she becomes pregnant with her first child.

It seems to me that practically no scientific treatment of this problem exists. Modern psychiatry, so far as it takes a sort of general notice of it, contents itself, as Krafft-Ebing does, with calling night wandering "a nervous disease," "apparently a symptomatic manifestation of other neuroses, epilepsy, hysteria, status nervosus."[2] The older literature is more explicit. It produces not only a full casuistic but seeks to give some explanation aside from a reference to neurology.[3] So, for example, the safety in climbing upon dangerous places finds this explanation, that the sleep walker goes there with closed eyes and in this way does not see the danger, knows no giddiness and above all is in possession of a specially keen muscular sense.

[2] Lehrbuch der gerichtlichen Psychopathologie.

[3] I introduce as the most important sources Peter Jessen: "Versuch einer wissenschaftlichen Begrdung der Psychologie," Berlin, 1855 (with many examples); Heinrich Spitta: "Die Schlaf- und Traumzust de der menschlichen Seele," 2d edition, 1882 (with abundant casuistic and literature); finally based upon these L. Lenfeld: "Somnambulismus und Spiritismus," Grenzfragen des Nerven- und Seelenlebens, Vol, 1900.

The phenomena of sleep walking and moon walking must be acknowledged, as far as I can see, almost entirely as pathological yet connected or identical with analogous manifestations of normal profound sleep. The dreams in such sleep, in contrast with those of light sleep, are characterized by movements. These often amount merely to speaking out, laughing, weeping, smacking, throwing oneself about and so on, or occasionally to complicated actions, which begin with leaving the bed. Further comparison shows the night wandering as symptomatically similar to hysterical and hypnotic somnambulism. This interpretation might be objected to upon the ground that unfortunately we know nothing of the origin of the motor phenomena of the dream and that understanding of the hysterical and hypnotic somnambulism is deplorably lacking. Still less has science to say about the influence of the moon upon night wandering. The authors extricate themselves from the difficulty by simply denying its influence. They bring forward as their chief argument for this that many sleep walkers are subject to their attacks as frequently in dark as in moonlight nights and when sleeping in rooms into which no beam of moonlight can penetrate. Spitta indeed explains it thus: "The much discussed and romantically treated 'moon walking' is a legend which stands in contradiction to hitherto observed facts. That the phantasy of the German folk mind drew to itself the pale ghostly light of the moon and could reckon from it all sorts of wonderful things, proves nothing to us." I can only say here that ten negative cases signify nothing in the face of a single positive one and a thousand-fold experience undoubtedly represents a certain connection between the light of the full moon and the most complicated forms of sleep walking.

Not merely does science avoid these things on account of their strangeness, but also the poets best informed in the things of the soul, whom the problems of night wandering and moon walking should stimulate. From the entire province of artistic literature I can mention only Shakespeare's "Macbeth," Kleist's "Prinz von Homburg," the novel "Maria" by Otto Ludwig, "Das Sudkind" by Anzengruber, "Jn Uhl" by Gustav Frenssen and "Aebel? by Sophus Michaelis.[4] Finally Ludwig Ganghofer has briefly sketched his own sleep walking in his autobiographical "Lebenslauf eines Optimisten," and Ludwig Tieck has given unrestrained expression to his passionate love toward this heavenly body in different portions of his works.

[4] The text of Bellini's "Nachtwandlerin" could hardly be called literature, nor Theodor Mundt's fabulous novel, "Lebensmagie, Wirklichkeit und Traum." The latter I will mention later in the text.

Only in "Maria" and in "Aebel? however do these themes play an important part, while in the other works mentioned they serve properly only as adornment and episodic ornament. I am not able to explain this unusual restraint, unless we accept the fact that our best poets shrink from touching upon questions which they themselves can so little understand.

It has been expected that the psychoanalytic method, which casts such light upon the unconscious, might do much to advance the understanding of the problems of sleep walking and moon walking. But unfortunately no one undergoes such an expensive and time-consuming treatment as psychoanalysis for moon walking, so that the hoped for illumination can come at the best only as a by-product in the psychoanalysis of neurotics. That has in fact been my good fortune twice, where I have been able to lift the curtain, though only a little, in two cases among my patients and also in individuals who were otherwise healthy. What I discovered there, I will relate in detail in what follows.

One point of view I will first set forth. Two questions appear to me to stand out among those closely bound with our theme. First on the motor side. Why does not the sleep walker, who is enjoying apparently a specially deep slumber, sleep on quietly and work out the complexes of his unconscious somehow in a dream, even though with speech or movement there? Why instead is he urged forth and driven to wander about and engage in all sorts of complicated acts? It is one of the most important functions of the dream to prolong sleep quietly. And then in the second place, What value and significance must be attributed to the moon and its light? These two chief questions must be answered by any theory that would do justice to the question of sleep walking and moon walking.

PART I

Medical

CASE I. Some years ago I treated a hysterical patient, exceedingly erotic. She was at that time twenty-two years old, and on her father's as well as on the mother's side, from a very degenerate family. Alcoholism and epilepsy could be traced with certainty to the third ascendant on both sides. The father's sister is mentally diseased, the patient's mother was an enuretic in her earlier years and a sleep walker. This mother, like her father when he was drunk, was markedly cruel and given to blows, characteristics, which according to our patient, sometimes almost deprived her of her senses and in her anger bordered upon frenzy.

The patient herself had been as the youngest child the spoiled darling of both parents and until her seventh year had been taken by them into their bed in the morning to play. In her first three years she always slept between the parents, preferably on the inner side of one of the two beds and with her legs spread, so that, in her mother's words: "One foot belongs to me and one to her father!" She was most strongly drawn, however, to the mother, toward whom at an early age she was sexually stimulated, already in her first year, if her statements can be relied upon, when she sat upon her mother's lap while nursing.

The little one early learned also that, when one is sick, one receives new playthings and especially much petting and tenderness, on account of which she often pretended to be sick purposely or she phantasied about dark forms and ugly faces, which of course she never saw, except to compel the mother to stay with her and show her special love and tenderness. Already in her second year she would go to bed most dutifully, "right gladly" to please father and mother and gain sexual pleasure thereby. The father then let her ride on his knee, stroked her upon her buttocks and kissed her passionately upon the lips. The desire after the mother became the stronger. When the latter had lain down and the little one had been good, then the child would creep to the mother under the feather bed and snuggle close to her body ("wind herself fast like a serpent"). The mother's firm body gave her extraordinary pleasure, yes, not infrequently it led to the expulsion of a secretion from the cervix uteri. ("The good comes," as she expressed it.) I mention convulsive attacks and enuresis nocturna, as pathological affections of her childhood which belong to my theme. The patient had in fact suffered in her first year a concussion of the brain, through being thrown against a brick wall, with organic eclamptic attacks as a result. The great love which she had experienced because of this led her also later to imitate those attacks hysterically. In the fourth year, for example, when she had to sleep in a child's crib, no longer between the beloved parents, she immediately produced attacks of anxiety in which she saw ugly faces and witches as in the beginning of the eclamptic convulsions. Thereupon the frightened mother took her again into her own bed. Later also she often began to moan and fret until the mother would take her in her arms to ward off the threatened attacks, and thus she could stimulate herself to her heart's content. As she reports, at the height of the orgasm she expelled a secretion, her body began to writhe convulsively, her face became red as fire, her eyes rolled about and she almost lost herself in her great pleasure.

Concerning her enuresis, in its relation to urethral eroticism, the patient relates the following: "When I pressed myself against my mother's or brother's thigh, not only 'the good' came, but frequently also urine with it. At about eight years old there was often a very strong compulsion to urinate, especially at night, which would cause me to wet my bed. This was however according to my wish to pass not urine but that same secretion which I had voided at two or three years old, when I became so wildly excited with my mother, that is when, lying in bed with her, I pressed her thigh between mine. I could not stop it in spite of all threats or punishments. Very curiously I usually awoke when I voided urine, but I could not retain it in the face of the great pleasure."

I lay emphasis upon a specially strong homosexual tendency[5] among her various perversions, although she had the usual sex relations with a legion of men with complete satisfaction. Furthermore, as sadistic-masochistic traits, there was an abnormal pleasure in giving and receiving blows and a passionate desire for blood. It was a sexual excitement that occurred when she saw her own blood or that of others. I have elsewhere[6] described this blood sadism and I will refer here to only two features, which are of significance also in regard to her moon walking. The first is her greatly exaggerated vaginal eroticism, which at menstruation especially was abnormally pleasurably excited. The second, on the other hand, was that our patient already at the age of two years should have experienced sexual pleasure in the mother's hemoptysis. Sitting on the mother's lap she stimulated herself upon the latter's breast, when she began to scrape and then to cough up blood. She reached after her bloody lips in order afterward to lick off her own fingers. As a result of the sexual overexcitement which occurred then, blood has afforded her enormous pleasure ever since, when she has looked upon it.

[5] This homosexual tendency was first directed toward her own mother in childhood and early puberty.

[6] "er den sado-masochistischen Komplex," Jahrb. f. psychoanal. Forsch., Vol.?, pp.?24-230.

As for the rest of her life, I will refer to two other points only, which are not without importance for our problem. First of all was the change of dwelling after the father's death in our patient's seventh year. The other is her burning desire, arising in her third or fourth year, to play mother and most eagerly with a real live child. A baby doll, of which she came into possession, was only a substitute, although for want of something better she carried this around passionately and did not once lay it out of her arms while asleep. At the age of eight it was her greatest delight to trudge around with a small two year old girl from the house and sing her to sleep as her mother had once done to her. "Carrying that child around was my greatest delight until I was fourteen years old."

I mentioned above that her mother had been sadistic and at the same time a sleep walker. "Mother herself told me that she also rather frequently walked at night. As a child she would wander around in her room without being able to find her bed again. Over and over again she would pass it without finding her way into it. Then she would begin to cry loudly with fright for her bed until Grandmother awoke and lifted her into bed. In the morning she remembered nothing at all about it.

"It was the same way with her desire to urinate. Every night she had a frightful need to urinate and hunted for the chamber, but, although it always stood in its accustomed place, she was not able to find it. Meanwhile the desire grew more severe, so that she began moaning fearfully in her sleep while hunting. She sought all over the room, even crept around under the bed without touching or noticing the chamber, which was there. Often she did not then return to her bed until Grandmother was awakened by her moans, brought her what she wanted and helped her to bed. It happened rather frequently that, because of the very great need, she wet the bed or the room while on her search, whereupon naturally a whipping followed. Sometimes she lay quite quiet later on in her sleep, but when she could not find her bed, was obliged to pass half the night in the cold room. Once when I myself wet my bed, she struck me with the words: 'Every time that this happens you will be whipped; my mother whipped me for this reason.' Although she knew from her own experience that it could not be helped, yet she struck me.

"Besides the moon exercised a great power over my mother. Since the house in which she lived was low and stood out in the open country, and there were no window blinds, on bright moonlight nights the moon shone into the farthest corner. In the corner stood a box, on which were a number of flower pots, figures and glass covers. Upon this box she climbed, after she had first taken down one object after another and placed them on the floor without breaking anything. Then she began to dance upon the top of the box, but only on bright moonlight nights. Finally she put everything back in exactly the same place to a hair's breadth and climbed out of the window, but not before she had removed there a number of flower pots out of the way. From the window she reached the court where she rambled about, climbed over the garden fence and walked around at least an hour. Then she went back, arranged the flowers on the window in exact order and--could not find her way to bed. There was always a scene the next day if Grandmother had been wakened in the night."

The most noteworthy feature in this statement, beside the phenomenon of sadism, later taken over by the daughter, the urethral eroticism and the susceptibility toward the moonlight, is the behavior of the mother while walking in her sleep. She plainly has an idea where the flower pots stand, which she removes from the box and the window, but on the other hand she comes in contact neither with the bed nor the chamber, which yet are in their usual places. We will also take note further on of the dancing upon the box in the bright moonlight as well as the climbing out of the window, climbing and walking about.

Before I go on with my patient's story, something should be said concerning its origin. She had been undergoing psychoanalytic treatment with me for nine months on account of various severe hysterical symptoms, which I will not here touch upon further, when she one day came out with the proposal that she write for me her autobiography. I agreed to it and she brought me little by little about two hundred fifty pages of folio, which she had prepared without any influence on my part, except of course that she had, in those months of treatment, made the technique of the analysis very much her own as far as it touched upon her case. Practically nothing in our work together in solving her difficulties was said of her sleep walking. I have also in no way influenced or been able to influence her explanation. It originates solely from the patient's associations and the employment of her newly acquired knowledge of the unconscious in the interpretation of her symptoms.

I find then in her account of her life some highly interesting points. "Even at two or three years old Mother at my entreaties must soothe me to sleep. As we lay together in bed I pretended often to be asleep and reached as if 'in my sleep' after my mother's breast in order to revel in sensation there. Also I often uncovered myself, again ostensibly in my sleep, and laid myself down quite contentedly. Then I awoke my mother by coughing, and when she awoke she stroked me and fondled me, and as was her custom kissed me also upon the genitals. Frequently I stood up in bed between my parents--a forerunner of my later sleep walking--and laid myself down at my mother's feet, asleep as she thought, but in reality awake only with eyes closed. Then I pulled the feather bed away from Mother and blinked at her in order to see her naked body, which I could do better from the foot than if I had lain near her.

"If she awoke she took me up to my place, kissed me repeatedly over my whole body and covered me up. I opened my eyes then as if just awakening, she kissed me on the eyes and said I should go quietly to sleep again, which I then did.

"Still earlier, at one or two years, I pretended to be asleep when my parents went to bed, that I might obtain caresses, because Father and Mother always said, 'See, how dear, what a little angel!' They kissed me then and I opened my eyes as if waking from deep sleep. This was the first time that I pretended to be asleep. I often lay thus for a long time apparently asleep but really awake. For when the parents saw that I was asleep, they told one another all sorts of things about us children. Especially Mother often spoke of my fine traits, or that people praised me and found me 'so dear' which she never said in my presence lest she should make me vain."

Here is an early preceding period when the little one deliberately pretends to be asleep in order to hear loving things, receive caresses and experience sexual activity without having to be held accountable or to be afraid of receiving punishment, because everything happens in sleep. In the same way similar erotic motives and analogous behavior may be found in the account of her other actions while asleep. As she began to talk at two years old her parents begged her to tell everything that had happened to her, for example in the absence of either of them. She must tell to the minutest detail, when she awoke early lying between her parents, what had happened to her during the day before, what she had done with her brothers and sisters, what had taken place for her at school, and so on. She responded so much the more gladly, because in narrating all this she could excite herself more or less as well upon the father's as upon the mother's body.

In fact, this was the very source of a direct compulsion to have to tell things, from which she often had to suffer frightfully. The very bigoted mother sent her regularly from her sixth year on with her sister to the preaching services with the express injunction to report the sermons at home. And although on account of her poor head she had to struggle grievously with every poem or bit of lesson which she had to learn for school, yet now at home she would seat herself upon a hassock, spread a handkerchief over her shoulders and begin to drone out the whole sermon as she had heard it in the church from the minister. And this all merely out of love for her mother! Furthermore she was, according to her own words, directly in love with her teacher in the school, who often struck her on account of her inattentiveness and certainly did not treat her otherwise with fondness. Here is a motive for the later learning, singing and reciting of poetry during the sleep walking, while the pleasure in being struck when at fault was increased by self reproach, that she in spite of all her pains was so bad at learning.

"During my whole childhood," the patient states, "I talked a great deal in my sleep. When I had a task to learn by heart, I said over the given selection or the poem in my sleep. This happened the first time when I was eight years old, on a bright moonlight night. I was sleeping at the time in the bed with my sister and I arose in the night, recited a poem and sang songs. At about the same period, standing on a chair or on the bed, I repeated parts of sermons which I had heard the day before at church. Besides I prattled about everything which I had done the previous day or about my play. How often I was afraid that I would divulge something from my sexual play with my brother! That must never have happened, however, or mother would have mentioned it to me, for she always told me everything that I said during the night." I might perhaps sum up this activity in her sleep after this fashion: Day and night she is studying for the beloved but unresponsive teacher and strives to win and to keep her good will as well as that of the mother through the repeating of sermons and relating of all the events of the day.

"As for the talking in my sleep, I began at the age of two or three, though awake, to pretend to be asleep and to speak out as if asleep. For example I acted as if I were tormented with frightful dreams and cried out with great terror, ostensibly in a dream: 'Mother, Mother, take me!' or 'Stay with me!' or something of the sort. Then Mother took me, as I had anticipated, under her feather bed and quieted me, but I naturally became excited while I pressed my legs about her body presumably from fear of witches and immediately there occurred a 'convulsive attack,' that is I now experienced such lustful pleasure that 'the good' came."

Attention may further be called to the fact that she threw herself about violently in her sleep, which caused her, as the daughter of so brutal a mother, who was herself a sado-masochist, an excessive amount of pleasurable sensation. When only two or three years old, as she lay between the parents, she pushed them with hands and feet, of which she was quite conscious, while they thought it happened in sleep. This brought the advantage that she was not responsible for anything which happened in sleep, for it occurred when she was in an unconscious condition.

The changing of the home in her seventh year, after the death of the father, led to her sharing the bed of her sister six years older than she. "My sister had the habit of throwing off the covers in her sleep or twisting her legs about mine. I, on the other hand, always hit her in my sleep with hands or feet. Naturally I could not help it since it actually happened while I was asleep, yet when my sister could stand it no longer I had to go and lie with Mother. I also struck her in my sleep. Besides I nestled up against her body, especially her buttocks, and experienced very pleasurable excitement. For it was simply impossible with her strong body and in the narrow bed to avoid touching my mother. Only I did it to her quite consciously, but she was of the impression that I pressed upon her in my sleep because I had no room in bed. The reason that I as a small child pushed against my parents in bed was simply the wish to be able to strike them once to my heart's desire, and since this was impossible during the day, I did it while asleep, when no one is responsible for what one does. Striking my sister then actually in my sleep, when I was seven years old, was again the wish to be able to excite myself pleasurably by the blows as when a smaller child." Here her sadism again breaks through in this desire to strike mother and sister according to her heart's desire and it especially excited her because of her constitutionally exaggerated muscle erotic. I have discussed this sadism at length elsewhere.[7]

[7] Cf. note?, p.?63.

It can be affirmed, if we examine her behavior in sleep, that without exception sexual wishes lay at the bottom of it, just as the dream also, as is well known, always represents the fulfilment of infantile wishes. The plainly erotic character is never wanting in an apparently asexual action, if we penetrate it more deeply. So for example this patient repeated the sermon at her mother's bidding in order to receive her love and praise. Saying her lessons at night arose from her strong attachment to her teacher, which again in turn was a stage of her love for her mother. Naturally this was all concerned with wishes, which, strictly tabooed when awake, could only be gratified in unconsciousness, somehow carried out in sleep, or, as with the simulated convulsions, only in the mother's bed. The behavior during sleep served especially well to grant sexual pleasure but without guilt or liability to punishment.

It was quite in order further that a conscious activity preceded the unconscious activity in sleep, that is, that for a time the patient while awake, but with closed eyes and therefore apparently asleep, did the very thing which later was done in actual unconsciousness. What then impressed itself as an unconscious performance during sleep, had been earlier done consciously, almost I might say as "a studied action." Only in special cases is there any need for playing such a comedy, for the direct demand of a beloved individual--"You must tell everything," "You must learn diligently," "Repeat the sermon accurately,"--when the eroticism is well concealed, permits of open action without more hindrance. It may be noted further that the patient never betrayed in the least in her sleep what she must have been at pains carefully to conceal, as, for example, the sexual play with her brother. Finally the striking participation of the muscle erotic at times in sleep must be emphasized.

We have found already as roots and motives of her sleep activity sexual, strongly forbidden wishes, which particularly could often be gratified only in bed; the striving that she might commit misdemeanor without being held guilty or answerable; further the practicing of these things first while awake; and finally, as an organic root, at least the pleasure in blows in sleep, the undeniably exaggerated muscle erotic. Nearly everything takes place in bed, only occasionally outside it, and then always near it. Complicated actions are completely wanting. Likewise nothing was said of the influence of the light or of the moon. Only in passing was it mentioned that the patient arose in the moonlight for her first nightly recitation of lessons.

The group of phenomena which we will now take up displays complicated performances and stands above all under the evident influence of the light of the moon. "In my fourth year," the patient relates, "I was put for the first time into a little bed of my own, so that my mother, who the day before had begun to cough up blood, should have more rest. She had closed the net of my crib and that I should not be frightened moved the crib up to her large bed. I pretended to be asleep and as soon as my parents had fallen asleep I climbed over the side but was so unfortunate as to fall into my mother's bed. I was quickly laid back in my own bed, without having seen the blood, which was my special longing. Often after this, almost every night, I tried again to climb into Mother's bed, so that finally she placed my bed by the wall in order to prevent my climbing over to her. For some months I slept alone in my little bed. She caught me one night, however, this time actually in my sleep, trying to climb over the side but entangled in the net. Fortunately I did not fall out but back into bed. At that time I produced also my pretended convulsive attacks that I might be taken by Mother into her bed and be able to excite myself upon her.

"Mother began raising blood again when I was ten years old and we had already moved into the new home. That year she was seized twice with such severe hemorrhages that for weeks she hovered between life and death. Then in my eleventh year I began my sleep walking. What urged me to it was again Mother's coughing of blood as well as the desire to see her blood, both reasons why I had already at four years old pretended sleep so that I could climb into Mother's bed."

The patient proved herself such an ideal nurse on the occasion of the mother's severe hemorrhage that the mother would have no one else. She watched tirelessly day and night together with her sisters, changing every few minutes the icebags which had been ordered. "Scarcely a moment did I tear myself away from my mother's bedside and, if one of my sisters relieved me, I often could hardly move, undress myself and lie down for an hour. If I did lie down, I threw myself about restlessly, torn with anxiety, and was only happy again when I sat by my mother's bed." This fearful anxiety was not however merely fear for the precious life of the mother, but still more, repressed libido. In spite of all her concern for the mother's suffering she could not prevent the strongest sexual pleasurable sensations at the sight of the mother's snow white breast in putting on the applications or when she raised blood. This intensive nursing lasted four weeks until finally a nursing Sister came to assist.

"As I now for the first time could enjoy a full night's rest, I fell into a deep sleep, as from this time on I always did before every sleep walking. Near my bed stood the table with Mother's medicine and on the window ledge, behind the curtain, a lamp, which threw its light upon my bed. Suddenly I arose in my sleep, went to my mother's bed, bent over her. Mother opened her eyes but did not rouse herself. Then the Sister, who was dozing on the sofa near Mother's bed, awoke and rushed forward frightened as she saw me there in my nightgown. She thought something had happened to Mother, but the latter motioned with her hand to leave me alone and to keep still. I kissed Mother and changed the icebag, apparently in order to see her breast. I could see no blood this time, so without a sound I moved away and went to the table, where I put all the medicines carefully together to make a place and then went out into the pitch dark kitchen without stumbling against anything. There I took from the kitchen dresser a bowl with a saucer and a spoon and came back again to the room. Next I seized a glass of water which stood there and poured the water carefully into the bowl without spilling more than a drop. With this I spoke out half aloud to myself: 'Now Emil (my brother-in-law, who had for a long time taken his breakfast with us) can come to his breakfast without disturbing Mother, who had always prepared it for him.' Then I went to bed and slept soundly for some hours, as I sleep only at my periods of sleep walking, without crying out. All that I have described the Sister of Charity told me afterward. Naturally I did everything with closed eyes, without knowing it, and moved about as securely in the darkness as if it had been bright day. The next morning they told me about it and laughed over it."

This is what she has to say of the influence of the light upon her sleep walking. "Here also Mother's coughing was the external cause as it had been when I was four years old. When Mother was ill, the lamp was left upon the window sill behind the curtain, burning brightly so that she would not be afraid. Now also, at the time of my first complicated sleep walking, such a light was burning behind the curtain throwing its light upon my bed and the wall. Mother had always left the light burning in order to see me at once, after I had sometimes climbed over the side of my crib at the age of four, when she was ill. The light however made me climb over to her, because in the dark no blood could be seen. Also when I began to moan, during my convulsive attacks, she made a light and came to my bed. Or she said, when my bed was pushed close to hers: 'Wait a moment; I will make a light and take you or you can climb over to me.' Next day I laughed with my parents over my visit at night, without suspecting that I would soon be repeating it actually in my sleep. And it was only for this, that I might, as at the very first time, enjoy the sight of Mother's blood. Now, when she had a light burning during her illness, this allured me in my sleep to climb out to her, as at that first time when she had made a light especially for me to climb over to her."

The following memory leads still deeper into the etiology: "Mother always had the habit of going from bed to bed, when we children were asleep, and lighting us with her lamp to make sure that we were asleep. I perceived the light in my sleep, which called me to Mother. She had lighted me that first time so that I might climb into bed with her. Now I thought in my sleep, when I saw the light, that she was calling me again and she found me often at the very point of climbing over to her. I see myself yet today with one foot over the bars, almost in a riding position. Yet nothing ever happened to me. A complete change took place within me when the light of a candle or a lamp fell upon my face. I might almost say that I experienced a great feeling of pleasure. I seemed to myself in my sleep to be a supernatural being. I immediately perceived the light even when I lay in deepest sleep. There was however no sign of waking. This must represent a second form of consciousness, which possessed me at such times. I often asked my mother all sorts of things while wandering about, always knew to whom I spoke although I did not see the person and before I heard anyone speak I already mentioned the person's name. My orientation in sleep walking was so exact that I never once stubbed my toe against anything. It was just so with urination, which was probably connected with the moon or with a night light accidentally falling upon me. As soon as I pressed out secretion or the urine came, I found myself in a half sleep without being able to prevent an excessive feeling of pleasure. Then first I came to myself. This seems to me to go back to the fact that Mother often awoke me on special occasions in the night, holding a lamp or a candle in her hand to set me on the chamber, especially when she heard me moaning in my sleep and suspected a convulsive attack."

In what follows a complete identification with the mother is reported in detail. That has come in part to our notice in the first sleep walking, when our patient prepares the breakfast for her brother-in-law. "After that first sleep walking when Mother was having hemorrhages, they took place now rather frequently, when the least glimmer of light fell upon me, when Mother, for instance, lighted a candle at night to take some drops for her cough. Thus it happened that almost every night, as long as our beds stood together, I acted this little part. Often my family did not awaken and yet we knew the next day, when something was missing, that I had been the culprit in my sleep, as the next little example will show.

"My greatest wish at that time, at ten years old, was to be 'Mother' and have a child that I might bring up as I pleased. One morning when Mother got up and wished to dress herself she did not find her underclothing. We sisters were still fast asleep and Mother did not wish to waken us. She could remember exactly that she had laid her clothing as she always did on the chair near her bed. When she saw that search was in vain she put on fresh linen. Fully an hour later I awoke and was completely astonished to find myself dressed and in Mother's clothing. The puzzle was now solved. The putting on of Mother's clothing during the sleep walking had plainly been merely my wish to put myself into the mother's place and also to play mother, as I did with the children day after day. It was just at this time that I was always seeking to trail around all day with children, whom I tormented, treated cruelly, often even struck them for no cause whatever, always with a great feeling of pleasure, as I myself fared at my mother's hands. It was very frequently the case that I spread the table for a meal, in Mother's place, or put on her linen or outer clothing. This happened most often when she was ill again with her cough or the light shone upon me in my sleep. The light of the candle was sufficient for this."

At thirteen years she began to be directly affected by the moonlight. "At that time I had to sleep in a small room which my brother had occupied before this. This room looked out upon the court and was, especially on the nights when the moon was full, as bright as if a lamp were burning in the room. I was very much afraid to sleep alone in a room. This was the first time in my life that it had happened. I feared that in every corner some one might be standing and suddenly step forth or might lie hidden behind the bed and although I first let the candle light shine over everything, I had no rest but was in continual fear. I slept here perhaps only fourteen days in all, but it was full moon just at this time and rather bright in the small room.

"Before going to sleep I always barred the door of the room, which near the other door of our house opened upon a small passage. On account of the shop we lived on an upper floor. When I lay in bed I was always thinking that I had not bolted the door well and every night I arose three or four times before going to sleep in order to make sure whether I had actually bolted the door carefully. This I did while awake. Finally I fell asleep. I knew nothing in the morning of what happened in the night. Yet for several days, when I arose in the morning, I found the door which led out of my room upon the passage standing open. I must also have gone about the house during the night, at least have been in the passage. It alarmed Mother and, when early the next day the door was once more open, she said that I need never sleep alone again. I had not had the remotest thought that she would watch me the next night. As usual she could, when I talked in my sleep, ask me about everything and obtain correct answers without wakening me. If however she called my name in fright, when I was walking, as in the scene about to be described, then I awoke. Some nights apparently I roamed about in the house, God knows where, in the moonlight, without any one noticing it. Now it was the window in the passage, which looked into the court and was always closed at night, that was left open. What took place there I cannot say, since no one observed me. I can however describe clearly what my mother saw happen and which she told me afterward.

"Before I lay down I tried the door several times to see if it were securely bolted, then slept until about twelve o'clock. Between twelve and one o'clock, when I as a child had always been most afraid because this was a ghostly hour, my mother, who compelled herself this night to remain awake, heard my door creak slightly. She watched and saw the following: I went out in my nightgown softly to the door and to the window on the passage, which I opened. I swung myself upon that rather high window and remained there a while without moving, sitting there while I gazed straight at the moon. Then-- it seemed to my mother like an eternity--I climbed down softly and went quietly along the passage into the first story. Half way along however I considered, turned back and went into my room. Having reached the door I turned once again and went along the passage to the door of the court. This was fastened. Again I turned and now went to the house gate. There I remained standing. I even tried to open it, as if I heard my name called. Then I was frightened, looked about me and was awake. Shaking with cold, for I was there half naked, I could scarcely orient myself. Then I crept to my bed and slept without waking.

"This happened in the second week. Every morning my door was open so that I had to sleep again in Mother's room. The moon never shone in there and the night light was covered. Nevertheless the sleep walking began also in this room in two weeks, if only the light of the candle fell upon me in my sleep. More often I lighted the candle myself in my sleep and went around in the room and the kitchen. Sometimes Mother found me standing by the door of the shop apparently about to open it and walk out. Now I have frequently, when I am lying in bed, the desire to spring out of the window, or to open both casements to get air for I am often afraid of choking. Mother had often felt this way in her illness. It also happened that Mother found me sitting by my chest, where I was looking for something which I had needed the day before and intended looking for the next day. I had laid out all my possessions about me. If Mother called me by name, I awoke; if she did not call me but only spoke in a certain way to me, I answered her everything without waking. I got up in my sleep, put on my mother's clothes, put on a cape and a nightcap, bade farewell to the children, to whom I wanted to be the mother, charged them to be brave and promised to bring them something. Then I took a piece of wood in my hand for an umbrella and walked about the room as if holding it opened out over my head because the sun shone. In reality it was the shining of the lamp. Mother's clothes were long and yet I wore the train beautifully and gracefully, without stepping on the skirt. My mother doubled herself with laughter when she saw such a caricature. Mostly I played the mother. Often I carried a small piece of wood wrapped in a cloth as a child in my arm and laid it on my breast. I sang songs, hushed at the same time other children--and knew nothing at all of it next day. Mother laughed most over this, that when I dressed myself, I first turned everything wrong side out. This goes back to the fact that Mother sometimes, when she had to get up in the night on my account and was half asleep, slipped her robe on twisted and wrong side out. These things lasted until my seventeenth year, when Mother was sick and I, as related above, made coffee in the presence of the Sister of Mercy.[8]

[8] I have here given word for word what the patient wrote down. When I then pointed out to her the evident contradiction, that she had misplaced something into the seventeenth year, which according to an earlier statement must have happened in the eleventh year, she answered that here was in fact an earlier mistake, since her brother-in-law Emil had first taken breakfast with her mother in her seventeenth year. The facts were these: She had walked a great deal in her sleep from her eleventh to her seventeenth year, for her mother had always suffered from hemoptysis, with occasional intermissions, and on this account had a nurse at various times. She had in

fact at eleven years done everything which she has described above, only the making of the coffee for the brother-in-law happened in the seventeenth year. Besides, all the other actions performed in sleep are correctly given. On being questioned, she stated that her menses occurred first between her thirteenth and fourteenth years and at the time of menstruation particularly she had walked a great deal. She was always very much excited sexually before her period, slept very restlessly and had always at that time arisen in her sleep. Blood always excited her excessively sexually, as has been already mentioned in the text. I will add just at this place that her exact dates, when an event appears in the very first years of her life, must be taken with a grain of salt, because falsification of memory is always to be found there. This, however, is not of great importance because the facts are authentically correct and at least agree approximately with the times specified, as I have convinced myself through questioning her relatives.

"Mother was rather often ill, so that beside the care of her, in which later a nurse assisted us, the shop had also to be looked after, which always demanded one person during the day. If I lay down upon my bed after two or three weeks of nursing, I fell into a deep sleep. This never hindered me however from being in my place to the minute, when my mother's medicine was to be taken. My mother could have anything from me, although I lay in a deep sleep. She did not need to speak, and if she wanted anything, she spoke it half aloud. The Sister, over weary from night watching, slept lightly, but if Mother needed anything, it was sufficient for her to breathe my name and I was awake, although otherwise I did not hear well and must always be aroused for some time before I was fully awake.

"In reality I merely imitated my mother in my sleep walking. In the first place it was my wish to hold some object in my arms during the night, or lay it near me, as if it were my child, to have one that I might play with it sexually. In the second place this went back to my early childhood when I lay near my mother and she played thus with me. In the third place it referred to a later time when I felt as a mother toward my doll, and never allowed it out of my lap by day nor out of my arms at night. When Mother wished to quiet me if I was suddenly afraid of ugly creatures at night, she had to make a light as quickly as possible. Then she took me upon her arm or laid me close to her. The light must however remain burning until I had fallen asleep so that the horrible faces could not torture me. As a child I often cried only for the light; it was the light that first completely quieted me. I longed indeed for the light that I might see the blood, and at the same time excite myself upon my mother."

The patient proceeds in her story: "This continued until the seventeenth year. At eighteen I had to go into the country because of a nervous trouble. There I was quite alone and also had to sleep alone in a room. I always went to sleep very late and once--my small room was bright with moonlight--I arose, went into the small passageway, which opened into the court, and was going out of the courtyard gate. I was obliged to turn back, however, because this was fastened. Yet instead of going back to my room, I went into the sleeping room of my landlady, who was sleeping there with her daughter, a girl of about twenty-six years. The moon was also shining into this room and I slowly opened the door. Both of them then awoke and were, as they told me next day, frightened to death. It affected the daughter especially, so that she was terrified and at once sought refuge in her mother's bed. I went back. What happened further I cannot say, for the daughter had immediately bolted the door behind me. I had made it impossible for me to stay longer in the little country village, and although I had paid for my room for a month I preferred to go away two days later. All the people avoided me and looked at me askance. Most of all the people with whom I was stopping! I saw that a stone rolled from their hearts when I departed." At my question, whether she perhaps had been especially attracted by her landlady, she answered: "No, but in fact with another woman of the village. And it seems that I at that time wished to go to this woman in my sleep walking. At least the landlady's room, into which I went, after I found the gate of the courtyard fastened, lay in the direction of the house where she lived.

"From this time nothing is known of my walking in my sleep even on moonlight nights. Only I have sometimes since that time put on my underclothes in the night, but always my own. That is I have often discovered in the morning, up till quite recently, that I had on my linen or my stockings. Besides I often dressed my hair during the night, and if I had had my hair, for example, braided or loose when I went to sleep, I would awaken in the morning with my hair put upon my head. This unconscious hair dressing happened most frequently before menstruation and was then an absolute sign that this would take place very soon. This has the following connection. Mother never went to sleep with her hair done up, but when in bed had it always hanging down in a braid. Only, when she was suffering from the hemorrhages--at the time of menstruation I also lost a good deal of blood-- she did not have the braid hanging down but put up upon her head. Before the appearance of menstruation this braid hanging down annoyed me very much. Furthermore, the doing of my hair in my sleep, which occurred a few days before, is only the wish again to see blood, for which reason it appears only usually before menstruation." I will add to complete this that the ceasing of her sleep walking at her eighteenth year was contemporaneous with her taking up regular sexual relations with different men.

The patient gives still other important illustrations of her awaking at the calling of her name by her mother, and of staring into the light, particularly the moon. "In school my thoughts were always on the sexual and therefore I heard nothing when an example was explained. I often resolved to listen attentively, but in a few minutes I was again occupied with sexual phantasies. Then if I heard my name called I woke up suddenly but had first to orient myself and think where I was. This awaking at the calling of my name at school was exactly like that when my mother called me by name during my sleep walking. Both times I was startled and awoke as if from a heavy dream. That excessive dreaming while awake goes back however to my earliest childhood, when I sat evenings on my mother's lap, while my parents were talking together, and excited myself with her. Oh, what wonderful things I dreamed! I always revelled then in sexual phantasies, and, completely lost in them, forgot entirely where I was until I suddenly heard my name called, when I started up frightened and had first to orient myself. Mother always called my name softly and usually added, when I began to yawn, 'the pillow is calling you,' and imitating a wee voice, 'You ought to come to it in bed.'"

Once more: "When evenings I began to dream on mother's lap, I was compelled to look directly into the flame of the lamp. I looked straight into it and was as if hypnotized. I laid both hands upon my mother's breasts and traced their form. Besides I had my braid lying upon her left breast, which I liked very much, because it lay as softly as upon a pillow. I was also compelled to look into the light, gazed steadily at the flame until my eyes were closed. Then I lay in a half sleep, in which I heard the voices of the family without understanding what was said. Thus I could dream best, until my mother called my name and I awoke.

"Every day I took delight in this sleep by the light of the lamp and the pleasure experienced upon my mother's lap. I lay quietly and with eyes closed so that they all thought I was fast asleep. Yet I knew indeed that it was no ordinary sleep, but merely a 'daydream,' from which I only awoke when Mother called me by name. When she did not do this, but quietly undressed me and put me into bed, I began to be restless. I stood up in bed, lay down at their feet and took care to cry out and throw myself about until Mother, quite alarmed, called me by name and quieted me. I believe that in these experiences lies another root for my staring at the moon when sleep walking, as well as for the dreamy state occasioned by the fixed gazing at the light."

In conclusion there are still some less important psychic overdeterminations. "I often had the desire, when looking at the moon at the age of four or five, to climb over the houses into the moon. I knew nothing at that time of sleep walkers. About the same time my sisters often sang the well-known song: 'What sort of a wry face are you making, oh Moon?' I stared immovably also at the moon, when I had the opportunity to look at it once from my window, in order that I might discover its face and eyes. Then, too, my eyes grew weary and began to close. Later, when nine or ten years old, I heard other children say that people dwelt in the moon. I would have given anything to know how these people looked, and whenever it was full moon, I gazed fixedly at it. I had understood that another people dwelt there of a different race. I wished to have another race of men. Perhaps they had other customs, thought differently, ran about naked as in Paradise and there I wished to go, and lead a free life with boys as with girls. Even as a child I seemed to myself quite different from the rest of humankind on account of my sexual concerns and sexual phantasies in school. I always believed that I was something peculiar and for that reason belonged not on the earth but upon the moon. Once when I heard the word 'mooncalf' and asked what it meant, some one at home told me that mooncalves were deformed children.

"I thought however that they did not understand; the children were quite differently formed, just as were all the people in the moon, so that their feelings were altogether different and they led a sexual life of a quite different kind. I thought they were kind to both sexes, because Mother always said, 'You must not be alone with boys!' and that in the moon this was permitted, for there no distinction was made between the sexes in play."

I asked her more particularly in conclusion whether her explanation for staring at the moon, that she identified moon and lamplight, was all there was of it. She answered immediately that another explanation had pressed itself upon her earlier, which she had rejected as "too foolish." "The moon's shining disk reminded me in fact of a woman's smooth body, the abdomen and most of all the buttocks. It excited me very greatly if I saw a woman from behind. Whenever I am fondling any one erotically and have my hand on the buttocks--I always think then of a woman--the moon always occurs to me but in the thought of a woman's body."

According to this explanation the sleep walker would have also stared at the planet, because the round sphere awoke sexual childhood memories of the woman's body, or, as I learned from another source, of the woman's breast, most frequently however of her buttocks. It is moreover noteworthy that it was always only the full moon that worked thus attractively, not by chance the half moon or the sickle. An everyday experience agrees very well with this. Children, when they see the full moon or their attention is called to it, begin to snigger. Every one familiar with the child psyche knows that such giggling is based on sexual meaning, because the little ones usually think of the nates. Not infrequently will children, when they are placed on the chamber, pull away their nightclothes with the words, "Now the full moon is up," likewise when a child accidentally or intentionally bares himself at that spot.

We have now the explanation, if we put together that which has just been told us, why our sleep walker wakes up on the spot and comes to herself as soon as she is called by name. This corresponds to her starting awake when in school she was recalled from her sexual daydreams and the earlier being startled when the mother called her out of similar sexual phantasies to go to sleep. The inference may be drawn from this however that one is startled from sexual dreaming also when the name is called during sleep walking, or going a step further, that sexual phantasies are at the bottom of sleep walking in the moonlight and first find their fulfilment here.

Could the interpretation of our patient be generalized, it might be said that the sleep walker climbs upon the roofs as a fulfilment of a childish wish to climb up into the very moon. It is of significance also how far we may consider universal her infantile belief that everything sexual is permitted upon the moon, that what was strongly forbidden her upon earth was there allowed to other children, and further the opinion that she was quite different because of her sexual phantasying and did not after all belong upon the earth but on the moon. At any rate the two motives introduced for staring at the moon's disk may be frequently met, are perhaps constantly present, that is the similarity of the moonlight and lamplight and the comparison of the moon's disk to the human body, especially the nates.

Let us attempt to realize now what this case before us may have to teach, the first and so far the only one of its kind to be submitted to a careful analysis. It must naturally be candidly confessed from the start that from a single case history, be it ever so clearly and fully set forth, no general conclusions may be drawn. Moreover certain factors resist generalization because they are of a more specialized character and at most will only occasionally reappear, as for example, the strong sadistic note, the desire for blood, the hemoptysis of the beloved mother. More frequently, also with the female sex, there may be the wish to climb into bed with the parents or their substitutes, to play the role of mother or father, out of love for them, and finally in general homosexuality may be a driving factor.

It is the sexual coloring and motivation of the sleep walking, especially by the light of the moon, which gives throughout the strongest tone to our case. This is something which the scientific authors have so far as good as completely overlooked, even where it has forced itself into view, as in a series of cases cited by Krafft-Ebing.[9] We shall hear, in discussing the works of the poets, that they and the folk place this very motive before all others, indeed often take it as the only one. We have here once more before us, if this opinion be correct, a scientific erotophobia, that is the dread--mostly among physicians and psychologists--of sexuality, although this is at least one of the chief driving instincts of human life.

[9] E, "A monk of a melancholy disposition and known to be a sleep walker, betook himself one evening to the room of his prior, who, as it happened, had not yet gone to bed, but sat at his work table. The monk had a knife in his hand, his eyes were open and without swerving he made straight at the bed of the prior without looking at him or the light burning in the room. He felt in the bed for the body, stuck it three times with the knife and turned with a satisfied countenance back to his cell, the door of which he closed. In the morning he told the horrified prior that he had dreamed that the latter had murdered his mother, and that her bloody shadow had appeared to him to

summon him to avenge her. He had hastened to arise and had stabbed the prior. Immediately he had awakened in his bed, bathed in perspiration, and had thanked God that it had been only a frightful dream. The monk was horrified when the prior told him what had taken place." The following cases besides: "A shoemaker's apprentice, tortured for a long time with jealousy, climbed in his sleep over the roof to his beloved, stabbed her and went back to bed." Another, "A sleep walker in Naples stabbed his wife because of an idea in a dream that she was untrue to him!" We may conclude, on the ground of our analytical experiences, that the untrue maiden always represents the mother of the sleep walker, who has been faithless to him with the father. The hatred thoughts toward this rival lead in the first dream to the reverse Hamlet motive, the mother has demanded that the son take revenge upon the father. Finally Krafft-Ebing gives still other cases: "A pastor, who would have been removed from his post on account of the pregnancy of a girl, was acquitted because he proved that he was a sleep walker and made it appear that in this condition??) the forbidden relationship had taken place." Also, "The case of a girl who was sexually mishandled in the somnambulistic condition. Only in the attacks had she consciousness of having submitted to sexual relations, but not in the free intervals."

There exists a better agreement of opinion over the relationship between sleep walking and the dream. Sleep walking, analogously to the latter, fulfills also wishes of the day, behind which stand always wishes from childhood. Only it must also be emphasized that the old, like the recent wishes, are exclusively or predominantly of a sexual nature. Because however that sexual desire is forbidden in the waking life, it must even as in the dream take refuge in the sleeping state, where it can be gratified unconsciously and therefore without guilt or punishment. Most of the sleep activities of our patient were performed originally in a state of apparent sleep, that is actually practiced in the conscious state until later they were carried out quite unconsciously. She would never then betray what when feigning sleep she had to conceal as causes. Finally the directly precipitating causes in her erotic nature for the sleep walking and moon walking seem especially to have been light and the shining of the moon, her puberty and her mother's sickness.

All of our patient's sleep walking, in accordance with the etiology and interpretation, since it goes back to infantile sexuality, is half sexual, half outspokenly infantile. It reaches the greatest degree, indeed the moon walking sets in just at the time of sexual maturity and leads to the most complicated actions before the menses, that is at the time of the greatest sexual excitement. And this activity in sleep and the moon walking too almost cease when the patient enters upon regular sexual intercourse. The shining of every light stimulates her sexually, especially that of the moon. The wandering about in her nightgown or in the scantiest clothing is plainly erotically conditioned (exhibition), but also the going about in the ghostly hours (see later), finally the being wakened through the softest calling of her name by the mother, with whom alone she stands in a contact like that of hypnotic somnambulism.

Purely childish moreover is the clever technique of disguise. First she simulates illness or fear in order to be taken into the mother's bed. Then she pretends to be asleep, talks in her sleep, throws herself about in her sleep, that she may be able to do everything without punishment and without being blamed, finally plays the mother in a manner which corresponds completely to child's play. Also later, before and after wandering in the bright moonlight, she produces specially deep sleep and first as if in an obsession tries the door repeatedly to see if it is closed. I see in this, naturally apart from possible organic causes of profound sleep, an unconscious purpose, which plainly insists: "Just see, how sound-asleep I am (we are reminded of the earlier pretending to be asleep) and how afraid I am that the door might be left open! Whoever has to walk about in spite of such sound sleep and such precaution, and even perhaps do certain things which might be sexually interpreted, he plainly is not to blame for it!"

We might add from knowledge of the neuroses that the fear that some one might be hiding in the room signifies the wish that this might be so in order that the subject might be sexually gratified. There was one circumstance most convincing in regard to this, which I will now add. Even during the time of her psychoanalytic treatment, when she did not wander at night any more nor perform complicated acts in her sleep, she had a number of times in the country carefully locked the door of her room in the evening, only to find it open again in the morning. To be sure, her lover of that period slept under the same roof, though at some distance from her.

Before I go more closely into the question as to what share the light had upon the sleep walking of our patient, I will recall once more that her actions during sleep were at first but few and had nothing to do with the light. As the years went by they became more complicated and finally took place only under the influence of the light, whether it was artificial or natural, that is of the moon. More extended walks were in general possible only in the light of the moon, which as a heavenly body shining everywhere threw its brightness over every thing, in the court, garden and over the street, while candles or lamps at the best lighted one or two rooms. The patient, given to sleep walking or moon walking, went after the light, which meanwhile represented to her from childhood on a symbol of the parents' love and gave hope of sexual enjoyment.

It was also bound inseparably within with motor activities of an erotic nature. When her mother approached her bed with the light it was a reminder to the child, Now you must go upon the chamber and you can pass "the good," or, when she sat on the mother's lap and gazed into the lamplight, Now you may stimulate yourself according to your heart's desire. Then the lamp was shining when the little one wished to climb into bed with the mother in order that, while exhibiting herself, she might see her as scantily covered as possible. And finally the striking of the light announced, "the mother is sick, in nursing her you will have the opportunity to see her bared breasts and her blood." Evidently the light thus led, when she climbed after it, to the greatest experience of sexual pleasure of her earliest childhood. On account of this strong libido possession the memory of the light was kept alive in the unconscious and it needed only that the light of the lamp or the candle should fall upon the face of the wanderer to permit her to experience in the most profound sleep the same pleasure, the unconscious was set into activity and everything was accomplished most manifestly according to the purpose that served her strong libido.

It is remarkable that our patient distinguished immediately a strong feeling of pleasure by the shining of every light, that moreover she seemed to herself as a supernatural being (glorification through the sexual feeling of pleasure[10]), that she herself imagined it must represent a second sort of consciousness, and finally that she stood in such contact with the beloved person as that of a hypnotized subject--somnambulist--with her hypnotist. For she perceived also the mother's lightest word when most soundly asleep, in spite of her difficulty in hearing at other times.

[10] One thinks of the halo in religious pictures, which indeed is nothing else than the shining of the light about the head.

What was the patient's intention in her longer walks under the moon's influence, that she, for instance, climbed to the first story, reflected for a moment and then started to go out at the gate? That becomes comprehensible when it is remembered that she once opened the door in her sleep for her lover in the country and furthermore in her first complicated sleep walking. The purpose of the latter has been stated, to climb into her mother's bed in order to obtain the greatest sexual pleasure. I do not believe I am far astray when I assume that this erotic desire of the child lies also essentially at the basis of her more extensive wandering in the moonlight. She simply wishes each time to go to the bed of some beloved one, which, as we shall hear later, is accepted by poets and the folk mind as a chief motive, and a fundamental one for many instances of sleep walking, especially with maidens.

It becomes clear now, likewise, why the patient climbs into the first story, then recollects herself and seeks to go out at the gate. In her seventh year she and her family had changed their abode and this had been before in the first story but was now on an upper floor. She is trying yet to climb into the mother's bed, this still remaining as a fundamental motive. Only she is not seeking the bed where it stands at the present time but where it stood in childhood, in the first story and in another house. She goes, therefore, downstairs but remembers, unconsciously of course, that this is not the right floor and wants now to go out at the gate to find the home of her childhood. Later in the country when she so thoroughly frightens her landlady and her daughter, there she is also going to a woman she loves and she leaves the house for this purpose and goes at least into the room that lies in the direction of the house where the beloved lies. Later still she opens the door wide in her sleep so that her lover can have free entrance.

We might also explain now in great part the sleep walking of the mother. As far as I can discover, the mother also as a very small child lived in another home than the one in which her sleep walking began. She ran about her room at night and could not find her bed and felt around in distress without coming upon the chamber, both of which stood in the usual places. This may be explained by the fact that in phantasy she was seeking the bed and chamber of her earliest childhood, which of course stood elsewhere. Moreover she attained by her moaning the fulfilment of her unconscious wish to be set by her mother upon the chamber and then lifted into bed. The wanderings in the moonlight, after which likewise she could not find her way back to bed, may be similarly explained, though I learned only this much about her dancing in the moonlight, that in her childhood she was very fond of dancing, which is also the case with our patient. Perhaps she wished also to play elves in the moonlight, according to poems or fairy tales or had, like her daughter, earned the special love of her parents through her skill in dancing.

We are now at the chief problem. How is it then that the night's rest, the guarding of which is always the goal of the dream, is motorially broken through in sleep walking? There is first a special organic disposition, which is absent from no sleep walker, a heightened motor stimulability[11]. This appears clearly with children, and so for example with our patient as a tendency to convulsive attacks, pavor nocturnus and terrifying dreams, from which she starts up.

[11] Cf. with this Krafft-Ebing, "Slight convulsions or cataleptic muscular rigidity sometimes precede the attacks."

As far as my observations go, it seems to me that there is a special disposition to sleep walking in the descendants of alcoholics and epileptics, of individuals with a distinctively sadistic character, finally of hysterics, whose motor activity is strongly affected, who also suffer with convulsions, tremor, paralyses or contractures. It should be merely briefly mentioned that the heightened motor excitability also establishes a disposition to a special muscle erotic, which in fact was easily demonstrable in every one of the cases of sleep walking and moon walking which have become known to me. The disturbance of the night's rest was made desirable through the satisfaction of the muscle erotic to every one for whom the excessive muscular activity offered an entirely specialized pleasure, even sexual enjoyment.

Moreover in our case a series of features besides those already mentioned bear undoubted testimony to the abnormally increased muscle erotic. I have already elsewhere discussed them in detail[12] and will here merely name briefly the chief factors. The patient had an epileptic alcoholic grandfather on the mother's side, who was notorious when under the influence of alcohol for his cruelty and pleasure in whipping. She had, besides a strongly sadistic mother, two older brothers, of whom the elder was frightfully violent and brutal, often choking his brothers and sisters, while the other found an actually diabolical pleasure in destroying and demolishing everything. Our patient exhibited already at two years old as well as through her whole life a pleasure in striking blows, and also conversely a special pleasure in receiving them, further at four years old an intensive delight in dancing, an enjoyment that was unmistakably sexual. We have learned above how she delighted to press herself upon her mother's body or twine herself about her legs. Moreover, finally, one of her very earliest hysterical symptoms was a paralysis of the arm.

[12] Cf. note, p.?63.

More difficult seems to me the answer to the second main question: What influence does the moon exercise upon the sleeper? It was earlier discussed, along with the various psychical overdeterminations, that the moonlight awoke first the infantile pleasure memories, among other things that that light shining everywhere lighted the way which led to the house and the dwelling of the earliest childhood. Mention was made of the infantile comparison of the moon's disk with the childish nates and perhaps the gazing upon the nightly orb, which seems besides most like a hypnotic fixation, may be also referred back to the same. Since we know today that the love transference constitutes the essential character of hypnotism, that symptom brings us once more to the eroticism. Beside there was not wanting with our patient a grossly sensual relationship. Finally there is also the infantile desire to climb over the houses into the moon, realizing itself in part at least in the moon-inspired climbing upon the roof.

Yet the second leading problem appears to me, in spite of all this, not completely exhausted. It might not thus be absolutely ruled out that more than a mere superstition lurks behind the folk belief which conceives of a "magnetic" influence by which the moon attracts the sleeper. Such a relationship is indeed conceivable when we consider the motor overexcitability of all sleep walkers and the effecting of ebb and flow through the influence of the moon. Furthermore no one, in an epoch which brings fresh knowledge each year of known and unknown rays, can deny without question any influence to the rays of moonlight. Perhaps in time the physicist and the astronomer will clear up the matter for us. Meanwhile the question is raised and can be answered only with an hypothesis.

In conclusion I have in mind a last final connection which the spell of the moon bears to belief in spirits and ghosts. It is established through many analyses that the visits of the mother by night form the basis of the latter, when she comes with the light in her hand and scantily clothed in white garments, nightgown, or chemise and petticoat, to see if the children are asleep or, if they are, to set a child upon the chamber. The so often mentioned "woman in white" may also be the maiden in her nightgown, who thus exhibits herself in her night garment to her parents as she climbs into their bed, later also eventually to her lover. The choice of the hour between twelve and one, which came to be called the ghostly hour, may perhaps be referred to the fact that at this time sleep was most profound and therefore there was least danger of discovery.

CASE 2. I introduce here a second case, in which to be sure the influence of the moon represented only an episode and therefore received also but a brief analysis. It is that of a twenty-eight year old forester, who came under psychoanalytic treatment on account of severe hysterical cardiac distress. The cause of this was a damming up of his feelings toward his mother, for whom he longed in the unconscious. His condition of anxiety broke out when he went to live with his mother after the death of his father and slept in the next room. He admitted that his father drank. Every Sunday he was somewhat drunk. Likewise the mother, who kept a public house, was in no way disinclined toward alcohol. He himself had consumed more beer especially in his high school days than was good for him. I would emphasize in his sexual life, as belonging to our theme, his strong urethral erotic, which made him a bed wetter in childhood, led in later years to frequent micturition at night and caused a serious dysuria psychica. His muscle erotic finally drove him to the calling of a forester.

Only the portions of his psychoanalysis, which lasted for eight weeks, which have to do with his sleep activities and his response to the moon will be brought forward. Thus he relates at one time: "At thirteen years old, when I was in a lodging house kept by a woman, I arose one morning with the dark suspicion that I had done something in the night. What I did not remember. I merely felt stupefied. Suddenly the boys who slept with me began to laugh, for from under my bed ran a stream of urine. In the night the full moon had shone upon my bed. We fellows had no vessel there but had to go outside, which with my frequent need for urination during the night was very unpleasant. Now there stood under my bed a square box for hats and neckties, which I, as I got up in the night half intoxicated with sleep, had taken for a chamber and I had urinated in it. This was repeated. Another time, also at full moon, I wet a colleague's shoe. They all said that I must be a little loony. When the full moon came, I was always afraid that I might do this again, an anxiety which remained long with me. I never dared sleep, for example, so that the full moon could shine directly upon me. Yes; still something else. Two or three years later the following happened, only I do not know whether there was moonlight. I was sleeping with several colleagues in a room adjoining that of the lodging house keepers, the man and his wife. I must have gone into them at night and done something sexual. Either I wished to climb into bed with the wife or I had masturbated, I do not know which. I had at any rate the next day the suspicion that something of the kind had happened. The landlord and landlady laughed so oddly, but they said nothing to me."

"Did your mother perhaps in your childhood come to look after you with the light?"--"Yes; that is so. My mother always stayed up for a long time and came in regularly late at night with the light to go to bed. My father was obliged to go early to bed because of his work and had to get up at midnight, when he always made a light." Here he suddenly broke off: "Perhaps it is for this reason that I have an anxiety in an entirely dark room. If there is not at least a bit of light I can not perform coitus."--"How is that?"--"I have remonstrated rather seriously with myself that the sexual act could be performed only with a light."--Then at a later hour of analysis: "When my father went away at night, I came repeatedly into my mother's bed. I lay down in my father's bed, also in a certain measure put myself into his place."--"Did your mother call you, or did you come of yourself?"--"I believe that my mother invited me to her. Now something occurs to me: The moonlight awoke me as my father woke me when he struck a light as he was going out. Then it was time to go into bed with my mother, for the father was gone, which always gave me a feeling of reassurance."--"Yes, when he was gone he could do nothing more to the mother. And then you could take his place with her."

Two months later came the following to supplement this: "Already in the grammar school I was always afraid someone might attack me in the night, because of which I always double locked the room and looked under the bed and in every chest. In childhood Mother came in fact to look after me and set me on the chamber."--"Then your neurotic anxiety presumably signifies the opposite, the wish that your mother shall come to you again."--"Or rather, I bolt the door so that my father cannot come to my mother. I followed in this also a command of my mother, 'Lock yourself in well!' She always had a fear of burglars. Now even since I have been living with my mother she has said to me more than once, that I should lock myself in well. But I thought to myself, 'What, bolt myself in!'"--"That would mean also that if the mother wants to come, only she should come."--"That is just what I thought to myself, when Mother woke me early, that she need not knock but come right in. In the daytime I lay in my mother's bed because her room was warmer than mine. I was feeling very wretchedly at that time and my mother said in the evening, 'Stay there where you are; I will sleep in the little room next. Leave the door open.' In the night I know I was very restless."--"Did you not perhaps have the wish that your mother should look at her sick child in the night, as she once did when you were younger?"--"Yes, to be sure. This wish pursued me and therefore I slept badly. I would have carried the thing out further if my dysuria had not hindered me. If I had arisen in the night or the morning, then Mother would at once have heard me in her light sleep and I would not have been able to urinate. One time I crept out of bed very quietly so that she did not hear me, and yet it held back a long time until I couldn't stand it any longer. It was just the same at the time when I was in the grammar and the high school, if Mother asked me to sleep near her and Father was not there. Then also I could urinate only with great difficulty. And now when I was living with my mother, I had the most severe excited attacks. There was no other reason for I was neither a loafer nor a drunkard. I have laid myself down in my mother's bed and been unwilling to get out. That is very significant. And if at any time I went away from home I at once felt so miserable that I must go back. I was immediately better when once there."

This case, when we consider it, is plain in its relationships. The excessive love for the mother is a decisive factor as well as the desire to play the role of the father with her. Therefore the fear of burglars at night, behind which hides in part the anxiety that the father would have sexual relations with the mother and in part the wish that the latter might herself come to him. Joined to this is the desire for all sorts of infantile experiences, such as the mother's placing him every night upon the chamber because of his bed wetting. In the later repression the pleasure in the enuresis as well as in the being taken up by the mother becomes a dysuria psychica. Naturally to the urethral eroticist in childhood, and also later unconsciously, micturition is analogous to the sexual act. In puberty the moonlight awakens him as in childhood the mother's light or that of the father. So on the one hand the memory of the former is awakened, who with the light in her hand reminded him to go to the chamber,[13] and on the other hand the memory of the going out of the father, which was a signal to him to go to his mother. He arises and carries out with her symbolically the sexual act, for he urinates into a vaginal symbol (box or shoe-vagina). Also the fact that he got up once by the light of the full moon and wanted to climb into the bed of the landlady, likewise a mother substitute, is all of a piece. This case here before us, as may be seen, confirms what the first has already taught us.

[13] In Rumania the folk belief prevails that children readily wet themselves in full moonlight. (Told by a patient.)

CASES 3, 4, and 5.--I wish to give further a brief report of three cases of walking by moonlight, which I regret to say I could only briefly outline in passing, not being able to submit them to an exhaustive analysis. In everything they confirm every detail of our previous conclusions.

The first case is that of an unmarried woman of twenty-eight, who walked in her sleep first in her sixth year and the second time when she was nine years old. "I got up when the full moon was shining, climbed over a chair upon the piano and intended to go to the window to unfasten it. Just then my father awoke and struck me hard on my buttocks, upon which I went back and again fell asleep. I often arose, went to each bed, that of the parents and those of the brothers and sisters, looked at them and went back again. Between sixteen and seventeen years old, when my periods first occurred, the sleep walking stopped." She adds later: "I frequently as a child spoke out in my sleep. My nose began to bleed when I was walking on the street and the sun shone upon me. After this the sleep walking improved. I always clung affectionately to my parents and brothers and sisters, and never received a blow except in that one instance by my father."--"Which you took rather as a caress, than as a blow for punishment."

In this case also the sleep walker plays sometimes the role of the mother, who satisfies herself that her dear ones are asleep. Moreover a period of talking in the sleep precedes the wandering by moonlight. It is noteworthy that the sleep walking is intercepted by a caressing blow from the father and ceases altogether when menstruation sets in. Also earlier nosebleed had a beneficial effect.

The second case is that of a forty-year-old hysteric, who in her marriage remained completely anesthetic sexually, although her husband was thoroughly sympathetic to her and very potent. Her father's favorite child, she strove in vain in early childhood for the affection of the mother, who on her part also suffered severely from hysteria, with screaming fits, incessant tremor of the head and hands and a host of nervous afflictions. This mother's daughters had all of them always an extraordinary passion for muscular activity with apparently great satisfaction in it. They were among other things distinguished swimmers and enthusiastic dancers. My patient besides could never tire of walking for hours at a time.

In our discussion she related the following to me concerning her sleep walking: "I got up once in the night when I was about ten years old. I had dreamed that I was playing the piano. I found myself however not in bed but standing between a chest and a desk scratching upon the latter with my nails, as if playing the piano, which finally awoke me. There was also a paper basket there which either I had stepped over or there was a space through which I could slip, at any rate the way there was not quite free. I stood in this narrow space and dreamed I was playing the piano. Suddenly I heard my mother's voice, 'Mizzi, where are you?' She called me several times before I finally awoke. Without it was not yet growing daylight, but the moon shone brightly within. I recollected myself immediately, realizing where I was, and went back to bed. I told my mother, as an excuse, that I had to go to the chamber." "Had you at that time a great desire to play the piano?"--"Three years later it made me sick that I had not had to learn, but then I had as yet no desire for music. We had no piano at that time. Yet among my earliest memories is that of the way in which my mother played the piano. As a woman I wished that I could express my joy and sorrow in music. I would mention further that my brother and my uncle on the mother's side[14] are both sleep walkers. The former always wants to come into my bed in the night when he walks in his sleep. I must emphasize that he is especially fond of me.

[14] They are both passionately devoted to sports, thus also endowed with a heightened muscle erotic.

"The following often happened to me after I was married but never in my maidenhood. I awoke in the night, sat up in bed and did not know what was the matter with me. I could not think consciously, I was quite incapable of thought. I knew neither where I was nor what was happening to me; I could remember nothing. I did not know whether I was Jew or Christian, man or woman, a human being or a beast, only stared straight ahead into the next room, at a point of light. That was the only thing that appeared clear to me. I held myself to it to regain clearness. I always said to myself: 'What, what then? Where, how and why?' My powers of thought went no further. I was like a newborn child. I stared fixedly at this point of light because I unconsciously thought I would obtain clearness there for everywhere else it was dark. This lasted for a long time until through the light I could distinguish what it was that caused the light. It was from a street lamp, so apparently before midnight, and the lamp lighted a bit of the wall in the next room. After I had said to myself for a long time 'What, what?' and stared straight at that light, I learned gradually to distinguish what made the light, that is to recognize, That there above, is a bit of lamplight; again after some time; That is my lamp. Upon this I recollected my home and then for the first time everything else. When I had made out the outlines of things around me, then returned the consciousness that I was a human being and was married. Of all that I had not before been aware. I do not remember that I had dreamed anything before this came on, or that anything had excited me, nor that anything special had happened beforehand. Beside nothing like it has ever happened to me when I have been greatly excited. At the most, after my marriage I led a life of strain. I was tied to a shop which was damp, unwholesome and full of bad air, and I am a friend of fresh air. I suffered very much mentally under these conditions, because I love light and air."--"Did you think that you were indeed not a human being?"--"No; only that with God's help I would endure this life." I will add here that her second sister also manifested similar disturbances of consciousness.

We find first in the foreground a family disposition to sleep walking and moon influence. The brother significantly always wants in his wanderings to get into the sister's bed, while our patient herself openly plays the part of mother, especially the mother of the earliest childhood. It is interesting also that when in her married life she had to give up her pleasure in light and air, the disturbances of consciousness set in, from which she could free herself only through fixing her attention upon a point of light. She had the distinct feeling that from this point of light things would become clear to her. One can easily think of occasions of being dazed by sleep when perhaps the mother came with the candle in her hand to see whether her child was asleep and the child awoke. The whole remarkable occurrence would then be simply a desire for the mother's love, which she all her life long so sorely missed.

Now for the last case, a twenty-three year old married woman suffering from a severe hysteria, who clung with great tenderness to her parents, but received a reciprocal love only from her father, while the mother preferred her sister. The patient told me of her moon walking: "I always wanted to sleep by the open blinds so that the moon could shine upon me. My oldest brother walked about in the night, drank water, went to the window and looked out, all of course in his sleep, then he went back to bed and slept on. At the same time he spoke very loudly, but quite unintelligible things and one could actually observe that the moon exercised an attraction over him. My younger healthy brother said that it was frightful, the many things that he uttered in the night. I also climbed out of bed one night when sixteen or seventeen years old, because I could not find the moon, and sought it and met my moon haunted brother. I immediately disappeared again going back to my bed and he did not see me.

"I was ill once, about the same time, with influenza, and continually repeated in my feverish phantasies that they should take down some one who was hanged and not punish him; he could not help it. There was moonlight at that time and moreover a light burned in the room. I took this for the moon, which I could not see but wanted to see. I strove only all the time to see the moon. The windows must be closed because I was afraid, but the blinds must remain open so that I could see the moon. Some one roused me then from my phantasies and there I saw that my cousin sat near me. He was not however the one hanged, it was some one who was first dragged out by another man, a warden in the prison. The face of the one who was hanging I did not see, only his body."--"Of whom did he remind you?"--"I do not know definitely and yet it was the cousin who sat near me. And as I awoke, apparently I called his name for he answered me, 'Yes, here I am!'"--"What about the warden of the prison?"--"A man is first locked up before he is hanged."--"Do you see also in phantasy something that hangs down?"--"Yes; when with my cousin I always had the desire to see his membrum stiff, as it could be felt and noticed outlined through his clothing." I will add likewise that behind the cousin and her sexual wishes toward him analogous phantasies toward the father were hidden. That which hangs down (pendens, penis) is also the phallus. Her adjuration that the hanged person should not be punished, he could not help it, is a demand for mercy for sexual sins (see also later).

"Upon the wedding journey my husband did not want to sleep by the open blinds, and I wanted to sleep nowhere else so that the moon could shine upon me. I could never sleep otherwise, was very restless and it was always as if I wanted to creep into the moon. I wanted, so to speak, to creep into the moon out of sight.[15] Recently I was out in the country with my sister and slept by the open blinds. The light from the heavens, to be sure not the moonlight, forced its way in and I had the feeling as if something pierced me,[16] in fact it pierced me somehow in the small of my back, and I arose with my eyes closed and changed the position of the bed, upon which I slept well. I knew nothing of it that I had arisen, but something must have happened because I now could lie comfortably.

[15] Phantasy of the mother's body? The moon's disk = the woman's body?

[16] A clear coitus phantasy.

"Something else still. About two years ago I observed the moon in the country, as it was reflected in the water, and I could not tear myself from this spectacle until I was suddenly awakened by my husband and cried out. Five or six years ago I went out in a boat upon the Wolfgang lake. The moon was reflected in the water and I sat there very still. Suddenly my brother, the one who is well, with whom I do not have much to do, asked, 'What are you thinking of?'--'Nothing at all.'--'It must be something.'--'No, nothing!' As we climbed out, I was still quite absent minded. Also at night I always had the moon before me and spoke with it."--"Consciously or in a dream?"--"I believe I was more asleep than awake. For if any one had come upon me then I should have felt it very painfully. I have incidentally noted the words: 'Oh moon with thy white face, thou knowest I am in love only with thee. Come down to me. I languish in torture, let me only comfort myself upon thy face. Thou enticing, beautiful, lovely spirit, thou torturest me to death, my suffering rends me, thou beautiful Moon, thou sweet one, mine, I implore thee, release me from this pain, I can bear it no longer. Ah, what avail my words and my complainings! Be thou my happiness, take me with thee, only pleasure of the senses do I desire for myself. Thou Moon, most beautiful and best, save me, take my maidenhood, I am not evil to thee. Draw me mightily to thyself, do not leave off, thy kisses have been so good to me.'" As may be seen, she loved the moon like a lover to whom she would yield herself entirely. The grossly sexual relationship is evident. It is after this fragment doubly regrettable that a penetrating psychoanalysis was not here possible.

The early sexual content of the moon desire and its connection with the parent complex is shown by her further statement: "Last summer in the country I had only my mother-in-law with whom I could talk. It was the time of the new moon and I could not bear complete darkness in my room. It was frightfully lonely to me thus and I could not sleep. I had the idea that in the lonely darkness someone was coming to me and I was afraid."

It soon came to light that she and her sister in their early childhood and again between the ages of eight and thirteen shared the parents' sleeping room and had repeatedly spied upon their sexual intercourse. Her present fear is also evidently the wish to put herself in the place of the mother, to whom the father comes. She recalls yet one more episode: "When I was nine or ten years old, the healthy brother was ill with typhoid and the parents were up nights on his account. We sisters were sent to stay elsewhere, where we had opportunity to play with a boy who carried on a number of sexual things with us. I then dreamed of him at night and phantasied the sexual things which I had done with him in the daytime. Apparently I had also at that time played underneath with my genitals. At the same time, while my brother had typhoid, I was unwilling to go to sleep and could not, because I could have no rest while my brother was ill." It is clear without further discussion to one who understands these things that it was not anxiety for the brother but secret, yet insistent sexual wishes which caused the sleeplessness. It is finally significant that, when later she dreamed of a burglar, he always came after her with a knife, or choked her, as her cousin and mother had often done to her.

As we consider this third case of moon affectivity we find again familiar phenomena, connections with early sexual dreams and the parent complex. Especially noteworthy is further her direct falling in love with the moon, to which she addresses her adoration in verses and to which she even offers her virginity. It is as if she saw in it a man, who should free her from her sexual need. One is reminded how in the first case, the one cured by psychoanalysis, the four-year-old girl sought continually the moon's face on the ground of a students' song. It could not, we regret to say, be ascertained, in the absence of a psychoanalysis, whether in this case the heavenly body represented to the moon walker some definite person or not.

CASE 6.--I add here three autobiographical reports, which I have gathered from literature. The first originates with the famous anatomist and physiologist Karl Friedrich Burdach, who from his tenth to his thirtieth year had occasional attacks of moon walking, although he apparently "enjoyed the most perfect health." "I have during these periods," he himself relates, "undertaken actions which I had to recognize as mine, merely because they could have been carried out by no one else. Thus one day it was incomprehensible to me why I had on no shirt when I awoke, and it remained so in spite of my utmost efforts to recollect myself, until the shirt was found in another room rolled together under a press. In my twenty-ninth year I was awakened from a night wandering by the question, What did I want? and then the consciousness of the somnambulistic state passed over in part to the awaking. First I found the question strange, but since I thought the reason for it would become plain, I need not betray it. Immediately, however, as I began to waken, I asked myself in what that consisted and, now that the somnambulistic state was over, the answer must be due me."

One cannot help finding this self revelation exceedingly interesting. The hiding of the shirt, although the affair is so incompletely reported, especially in its motivation, points unmistakably at least to exhibitionism. The second sleep walking appears much more difficult of explanation. In this Burdach sought plainly a definite goal, which seemed so clear and transparent to him that he could not at all understand why anyone should question him about it. If we consider that his first thought on waking was that he need not betray this purpose, that moreover there enters at once a repression and causes him completely to forget it, there remains then no other possibility than that we have to do with a strongly forbidden wish, which the conscious censor will not allow to pass. It is easy to conceive a sexual motivation in this second instance if we remember that in the first sleep walking something sexual surely took place.

Still more probable is the strongly forbidden sexual goal, if we take into consideration the circumstances of his life. In his autobiography "Rukblick auf mein Leben" Burdach tells us how extraordinarily his mother depended upon him. "Having already lost four children in their first year, she had longed to bear another child and especially since the setting in of the illness of my father had compelled her to think of losing him, she had wished for a son as a sure object for her love-thirsty heart. Her wish was fulfilled when she bore me." Eleven months later the father died, leaving his wife and his little son not yet a year old unprovided for. Nevertheless she, the widow, rejected the proposal to return to her parents' home and preferred rather "trouble, need and a thousand cares upon herself in order that I might be better educated; for I was the object of her deepest love. About nine o'clock in the evening she went with me to bed and twined her arm about me; in the morning she stole from my side and permitted me an hour or two more of rest (p. 14).

"Women had a particular influence upon me; but it was also natural to me to attach myself to them. As my mother related, I never as a child went for a ride on my hobby horse without having at parting and on my return kissed my hand to my lady represented by a doll" (p. 24). It is superfluous to add that this lady was no other than his mother. Also the following passage I think is significant: "I was by nature endowed with as great a sensitiveness to womanly charm as to womanly dignity and this inclination toward the other sex grounded in my psychical constitution was nurtured by circumstances from my earliest youth on. I could but recognize very soon the high intellectual and moral quality of my good mother, who in her struggle with poverty kept herself fresh and free from vulgarity and shunned no sacrifice for me. Likewise the matrons to whose well wishing I owe my gratitude, inspired me with high respect for their character. In my former nurse there seemed to me a pattern of tireless and sagacious activity of a high order and breeding.... Thus a high respect for true womanhood was implanted in me. On the other hand I was as a boy made so accustomed to this role by several young women, who entertained themselves with me and considered me as their lover to while away their time, that I later retained the inclination to play this part and considered a friendly advance as an invitation which I in turn held as a sacred claim of honor and an agreeable duty" (pp. 69 ff.).

When later the mother took a young widow into lodgings, the young man, then twenty-one years old, had "the exalted feeling of being her protector. Then it was all up with my heart" (p. 71). The death of the dearest one to him on earth, his mother, followed close upon this and brought an end to it. "I became convinced that happiness would be found for me only where I shared it with another being, and that I could be satisfied only by a relationship similar to that in which I had stood toward my mother; an inner bond where only a single mutual interest controlled, where one soul found its happiness only in the other. Without such an absolute love, penetrating the whole being, life seemed to me worthless and stale. My mother, whose unbounded love I had enjoyed, was torn from me; my excellent uncle, heartily devoted to me, I saw in the enjoyment of his own family happiness. And an unconquerable desire for the same happiness tortured me as I felt my utter loneliness" (p. 79). So he concluded to marry although he had only limited prospects for supporting a family.

"The first intimation that my wife was pregnant filled me with delight. I took it for granted that Heaven would send me a daughter. With my idea of the value of woman all my wishes tended thither, to possess a daughter and to be able to watch over her while she unfolded to a noble womanhood. She should have my mother for her pattern and therefore also be named Caroline after her.[16a] I spoke so confidently, after I had left Vienna, of 'our daughter Caroline' in my letters to my wife that she was finally quite concerned and sought to prepare me for the birth of a son. I had not however made a mistake and my confidence was in the end justified" (pp. 83 ff.). His wife was confined at some distance from him and then as soon as possible journeyed to him with the little one. He relates as follows: "I went in Borsdorf with a beating heart to the carriage which brought her to me, kissed her hastily, took my child out of her arms and carried it hastily into the inn, laid it upon the table, loosed the bindings which bound it to its tiny bed and was lost in happy contemplation of the beautifully formed, lovely, vigorous and lively little girl and then first threw myself into the arms of my wife, who in her mother's pride and joy was feasting her eyes upon us, and then I had again to observe the lovely child. What cared I for mankind! What cared I for the whole world! I was more than happy" (pp. 85 ff.).

[16a] Cf. Barrie: "Dear Brutus," Act.I. for the dream daughter, who bears the name of the author's mother. See also "Margaret Ogilvy." The dream daughter's apostrophe to the moon is also interesting in connection with the present study. Tr.

The manner also in which he brought up his child is highly significant: "Our hearts clung mostly to our daughter.... I enjoyed the pleasure of possessing her with full consciousness of her worth, gazed upon her with rapture and was delighted when I observed in her a new trait of beautiful womanly character. She recognized by my serious treatment of her the entire depth of my love, repaid it with inner devotion and challenged it with merry playfulness. From her first year I delighted to lift her from her bed in the morning and even when she was eight years old she often got up of herself, knocked on the window of the alcove door leading into my work room and whisked back to her bed, so that when I came she could throw herself with hearty laughter into my arms and let me take her up. Or she slipped behind my chair and climbed up behind my back, while I was deep in my work, so that she could fall triumphantly upon my neck.

"I must refrain from mentioning more of her winsome childhood. She was the most beautiful ornament of my life and in the possession of her I felt myself, in spite of all pecuniary need, immeasurably happy." It will not surprise any one with knowledge of these things that a child so insatiable for love should become hysterical. "Her sensitiveness was unnaturally exaggerated," also she was seized once with a hysterical convulsion, as Burdach relates. She died young and "the flower of my life was past. The fairest, purest joy was extinguished for me. I had wished her for myself and Heaven had heard me. Finding in her the fulfilment of my warmest wishes, I had never thought it would be possible that I should outlive this daughter. Nevertheless I bore the pain ... confident of being reunited with her.... For thirty years scarcely a day has passed on which I have not at least once thought in my inmost soul of my Caroline" (pp. 142-147).

I will cite in conclusion still one more fragment of self characterization: "A chief trait in my character was the need for love, not that everyday love which limits itself to a personal pleasure and delight, but that unbounded, overflowing love which feels itself completely one with the beloved.... The ideal of marriage was before me in youth, for this need for love has been mine all my life.... I remember as a student having written in my diary that I would rather forego life itself than the happiness of family life" (pp. 53 ff.).

The center of this interesting life is Burdach's deep oneness with his mother. She on her part took him from the beginning unconsciously as a sexual object, as a substitute for her husband, who was failing in health and soon after died. She lay in bed near her little one, her arm twined about his body and slept with him until morning. No wonder that the boy was so sensitive to womanly charm and likewise that later different women looked upon him as their lover. The thought early established itself with Burdach that only such a relationship could satisfy him as that in which he had stood toward his mother. And as he stood for the father it seemed to him a certain fact that now a little girl should come to be the surrogate for his mother. Noteworthy also is his attitude toward the mother who had just been confined and the child. The former is to him almost incidental, while in the contemplation of his child, in whom he secures his mother again, he can scarcely get his fill, and he overwhelms her later with such passionate love as he had once obtained from his mother. When the girl was torn from him, he was consoled only by the thought of being united again with her in heaven.

We may see finally in the fond play in bed with his daughter a repetition of that which he carried on with his mother, and we may remember also that as a child he always slept with his mother. From all this it seems to me a light falls upon the unexplained purpose of Burdach's sleep walking. If this seems completely clear to him but so objectionable that he not only concludes to keep it secret, but, more than that, forgets it on the spot, then the probability is, that he desired that night to climb into bed with his beloved mother.

CASE 7. A second autobiographical account of repeated sleep walking I find in the "Buch der Kindheit," the first volume of Ludwig Ganghofer's "Lebenslauf eines Optimisten." When the boy had to go away to school his mother gave him four balls of yarn to take with him, so that he might mend his own clothing and underwear. She had hidden a gulden deep within each ball, a proof of mother love, which he later discovered. In the course of time while at the school the impulses of puberty began to stir in him and pressed upon him so strongly at first that frequent pollutions occurred. He thought he must surely be ill, until finally a colleague explained to him that this was on the contrary a special sign of health. This calmed him and now he could sleep splendidly.

"One night I awoke suddenly as if roused by a burning heat. I experienced a horrible suffering and believed I felt a hand on my body. I cried out and pushed with my feet, and as I lay there in a half consciousness it was as if many of my dormitory companions were awake and I heard them ask, 'What is it? Who has called out this way?' A voice, 'Some one has been dreaming!' And another voice, 'Silence in the dormitory!' And all was gone from me as if under a heavy veil. Once again quiet. Am I asleep or am I awake? A wild beating in the arteries of my neck, a roaring in my ears. Yet in the dormitory all is quiet. The lamp is burning, I see the white beds. I see the copper of the washstand glimmer like red gold. Must I have dreamed--an oppressive, frightful dream? Drops of sweat stood out on my forehead. Then came a heavy sleep. What was this? I rarely had days of depression or restless, disturbed nights. And yet in these weeks I entered upon this uncomfortable experience.

"One night I awoke. Darkness was round about me. And I was cold. And I saw no lamp, no bed, no shining copper. Was this also a dream? Yet my hands felt plainly the hard wood in front of me. Slowly I recognized a number of vaguely outlined squares, the great windows. Clad only in my shirt, I sat in the study room before my desk. Such a horror fell upon me as I cannot describe. I ran wildly up the stairs, threw myself into my bed and shook. Another night I awoke. Darkness was about me. Again I was cold. And I believed that I was again sitting at my desk. No; I was standing. My hands however felt no wood, my eyes found not the gray windows. As I moved, my head struck against something hard. I became aware of a feeble light shining. As I went towards it, I came from some dark room upon the dimly lighted stair landing.

"I awoke again in the night. I was cold. A semi-darkness was about me and over me many stars twinkled. I sat upon the shingle roof of the bowling alley. It was not a far leap to the ground below. But the pebble stones of the seminary garden pricked my bare feet. Moreover, when I wanted to get into the house, I found the gate closed. My God! how had I then come out? Somewhere I found an open window and climbed into the house and noiselessly up to the dormitory. The window near my bed stood open--and there outside, I believe, was a lightning rod.

"All day I racked my brains to find a way to escape from the fear of this dreadful thing. I dared not confide in anyone, for fear of the ridicule of the others, for fear--I never knew just what I feared. In the evening I took one of Mother's balls of yarn to bed with me, bound two double strands about my wrists and tied the ends around the knobs of the bedstead. In the night, as I was about to wander again, I felt the pull of Mother's threads and awoke. It never came again. I was cured."

This appears at the first glance a non-sexual sleep walking. This is only however in its first appearance, although it is to be regretted that the full explanation can scarcely be given in the absence of any analysis. It is first to be noted that sleep walking sets in at puberty and is ushered in by anxiety dreams, pollutions and various anxiety equivalents. The hammering in the arteries, the roaring in the ears, the restless, disturbed nights, as well as the unusually disturbed days, we know these all as manifestations of an unsatisfied libido. The first "frightful" anxiety dream seems to lead deeper, as well, as the "horrible suffering" started by a hand, which he felt upon his body. Must not this hand, which causes this "horrible suffering" to the youth who had never yet known trouble, have touched his genitals?[17] Behind this perhaps, moreover, are very early memories of the care bestowed upon the nursing infant and the child.

[17] One may also think of the fear of castration, associated with the threats of parents so very frequently made when children practice masturbation.

The terror which fell upon him every time that he walked in his sleep is worthy of note, for he was not otherwise easily frightened. "A terror which I could not describe," "fear of that dreadful thing" and fear not merely of the ridicule of his fellows but of something, what, he never knew, which is a far more violent reaction than we have been accustomed to find with sleep walkers. This excessive reaction may be very well understood, however, if behind it a particularly inacceptable sexual factor hides itself. Finally the cure by means of the mother's balls of yarn, homely proof of her love, doubtless has to do with the erotic. It must be admitted to be sure that we have to confine ourselves to mere conjectures. Only one may well maintain that even an apparently non-sexual case soon reveals its sexual grounding. Moreover, a strong muscle erotic is demonstrated further throughout Ganghofer's autobiography.

CASE 8. I will now, especially upon the subject of moon walking, cite an author who shows a very unusual preference for this heavenly body. In many a description and in many of the speeches which he has put into the mouths of his heroes, has Ludwig Tieck, who also has sung of the "moon-lustered magic night," given artistic expression to this quite remarkable love mania-- this is the correct designation for it. Ricarda Huch in her "Blezeit der Romantik" makes the striking statement that from this poet's figures one must "tear away the labels stuck upon them and name them altogether Ludwig Tieck, for in truth they are only refractions of this one beam." One may hear for example how Sternbald felt: "The orb of the moon stood exactly opposite the window of his room." He watched it with longing eyes, he sought upon the shining disk and in the spots upon it mountains and forests, wonderful castles and enchanted flowers and fragrant trees. He believed that he saw lakes with shining swans which were drawing boats, a skiff which carried him and his beloved, while about them charming mermaids blew upon their twisted conchs and stretched their arms filled with water lilies over into the bark.

"Ah, there, there!" he would call out, "is perchance the home of all desire, all wishes; therefore there falls upon us so sweet a melancholy, so soft a charm, when that still light, full and golden, floats upon the heavens and pours down its silver light upon us. Yes, it awaits us and prepares for us our happiness, and for this reason its sorrowful look toward us, that we must still remain in this earthly twilight." The similarity here with the phantasies of the psychoanalytic patient at the beginning is indeed unmistakable.

Yet one or two extracts from the novel "Der Mondshtige,"[18] the title of which is misleading since it in no way treats of one afflicted with lunacy but of a veritable moon lover, presumably our poet himself. There the nephew, Ludwig Licht(!), writes to his uncle: "It is now three months since I had a very serious quarrel with my friend, a quarrel which almost separated us, for he mocked at an entire world which is to me so immeasurably precious. In a word, he railed at the moon and would not admit that the magic light with which it shines was anything beautiful or exalting. From Ossian to Siegwart he reviled a susceptibility toward the moon although the poets express it, and he almost had declared in plain words that if there were a hell, it certainly would be located in the moon. At any rate he thought that the entire sphere of the moon consists of burned out craters, water could not be found upon it, and hardly any plant life, and the wan, unwholesome reflection of a borrowed light would bring us sickness, madness, ruin of fruits and grains, and he who is already foolish will without doubt behave himself worst at the time of full moon.... What concern is it of mine what the astronomers have discovered in the moon or what they will yet discover?... It may be ludicrous and vexatious to devote oneself exclusively and unreservedly to this or that, any observation, any favorite object. Upon my earlier wanderings I met a rich Englishman who traveled only to waterfalls and battlefields. Ridiculously enough, though I have not journeyed only in the moonlight, yet I have from my earliest youth forever taken note of the influence of its light, have never in any region missed the light of the full moon and I dream of being, not quite an Endymion, but yet a favorite of the moon. When it returns, its orb little by little growing full, I cannot suppress a feeling of longing while I gaze upon it, whether in meadow and woodland, on the mountains or in the city itself and in my own room."

[18] Literally, "Moonsick." [Tr.]

And the uncle answers him: "It is true, you are moon sick, as we have always called you, and to such a one much must be forgiven which would have to be reckoned differently to a well man. I have myself however always inclined to this disease." In fact the entire action, loving and losing, the development and solution of the plot, takes place almost exclusively under the light of the moon. At the conclusion, when the hero finds the beloved given up for lost, he cannot refrain from the outcry: "Yes, the moonlight has given her and led her to me, he, the moon has so rewarded me, his true friend and inspired panegyrist!" I regret that I find nothing in the biographies which would explain Tieck's exquisite amorousness toward the moon.

PART II

Literary Section

It is my purpose to bring also our beautiful literature to the solution of the exceedingly difficult and obscure problem of sleep walking and moon walking.

Our poets, for all our psychiatrists and psychologists, possess the finest knowledge of the psyche and during the centuries before science was able to throw light upon the puzzles of the mind, they solved them prophetically with discerning spirit. Thus they knew how to bring to light various elements of our problem. Their creations directed to that end arose from their own inner nature, through analogy, or because sleep walking was not foreign to them themselves. And even if neither were the case, they still had the ability of those who have a real true knowledge of men, quite intuitively to see clearly into the unconscious of others. We will come to know what profound interest many of the great poets, like Otto Ludwig and Heinrich von Kleist took in night wandering and moon walking and how they have first introduced these dark problems into other traditional material. A striking similarity is revealed if one compares that which the poet has in mind with that which I have been able to report in the medical section. I shall be able satisfactorily to verify the statement that science and art have reached exactly the same result. First however I will present the examples from the poets according to their comprehensibility and their transparency. I begin with

"AEBEL?" by Sophus Michaelis.

Twice had Soelver drawn near to the maiden Gro, daughter of his neighbor, Sten Basse. The first time was when in the spring he visited the island Aebeloe, which belonged to him but was quite uninhabited. So bright the day and so warm the kiss of the sun upon him, yet suddenly it was "as if his bare neck were flooded by a still warmer wave of light." A maiden stood before him, "who was like pure light. The eyes were as if without pupils, without a glance; as she looked it was as if white clouds floated forth out of a heavenly blue background. Soelver sprang up and stood face to face before her. Her cheeks grew red. Although unknown to each other, they smiled one at the other like two seraphim. Her hands opened toward his and before her, as out of her lap, fell the flowers which she had gathered. Soelver believed for a moment that it was all a dream. He swung his hands into the air and a hand waved toward him. He closed his eyes that he might enjoy to the full the soft, fleeting impression. It floated over his hand like an incorporeal breath. Was it then a ghostly vision, that wandered there at his side!" When however he knew that the maiden near him was a living being, then "his lips sank toward her trembling with desire, unintentionally and yet irrevocably." At this moment a "cloud passed over the sun and the light became at once dulled as if a mist had fallen upon all the flowers. Of all this he did not become so quickly aware, as that his own cheeks resounded from a whizzing blow." Her face glowed bright with anger and the delicate blue veins were swollen on her forehead, while with a scornful look she turned her back to him. His blood was however aflame with desire for revenge.

A second time had the young nobleman Soelver sought to satisfy his masculine passion, when he surprised Gro bathing upon Aebeloe. She however had defended her maidenhood and struck him about the head with an old, rusty sword, which she found on the shore, so that he sank upon the grass covered with blood. "He felt the pain of his wounds with a strange glow of pleasure. The blow had fallen upon the hard flint stone within him so that the sparks of passion had sprung forth. He loved the maiden Gro. A consuming passion raged in his blood. In his thoughts he knelt always before that ineffaceable image, which struck him to the earth with a flame of divine wrath in her eyes." In revenge for the trespass committed Sten Basse fell upon Soelver's castle and took the young nobleman himself prisoner.

Wild violence of this sort was indeed familiar to Sten Basse. He himself had once taken his wife thus by force. Just as he was flattering himself that he had broken her will once for all, she bit him in his chin so that the blood gushed forth and she spit his own blood into his eyes. He was struck with admiration at such strength. He had thought to desert her at once. Now he lifted her in his arms, carried her from her father's castle into the stable, bound her to his horse and rode forth--to his own home. Their marriage had been at first a long series of repetitions of the first encounter. In the end she loved him as the horse loves the iron bit between his teeth and the spur in his flank. She did not allow herself to be subdued by the blows which he gave her, but she was the weaker and she loved him because he was strong enough to be the stronger. An evil fate had taken his sons from him one after the other. Therefore he wished to call forth in his only daughter the traits of his own blood, his pride, disdainfulness and stiff-neckedness. "She must know neither fear nor weakness; her will must be hardened and her courage steeled like that of a man. When he heard that his daughter had been in danger but had saved herself, he swore revenge to the perpetrator of the outrage, yet at the same time his heart laughed with pride at Gro's fearlessness. He took the young nobleman prisoner and rewarded him with heavy and tedious torture as penance for his insolence. Yet at the same time he delighted himself with the thought of putting his daughter to a still more dangerous proof. He wished to see the young-blooded, inexperienced birds reach out swinging and scratching in attack and defense."

As if in mockery he gave to the imprisoned youth the passionately desired Gro to be with him in the dungeon. "She stood there as if she had glided into his prison by the flood of light entering in and he trembled lest the light would again absorb her into itself." He knew not what power forced him to his knees and threw him at her feet with a prayer for forgiveness. She had however merely a scornful laugh for the man humbling himself in his love and the cruelly abusive word, "Creeping worm!" Then in his sense of affront there comes the thought that Gro was given into his power. While he tried the walls of his dungeon to ascertain if he was perhaps watched, Gro stood and stared out by the aperture through which the light entered, now paler than before. Soelver stepped near her, drew the single gold ring from his finger, which had come down to him through many generations of his forefathers, and extended it to her as a bridal gift. But she threw it unhesitatingly out through the peephole.

Now bitterness raged in Soelver's blood. "He bowed himself before her face in order to intercept her gaze, but he did not meet it though her eyes were directed toward his. It was indeed no glance but a depth into which the whole light of day, which was blue now without overhead, was drawn down into a deep well. Soelver became intoxicated with this light, which, as it were, appeared to seek her alone and threw an aureole of intangible beauty about her form." He crept up and pushed forward the wooden shutter, then carried Gro to his cot. "She had let herself go without resistance and fell lifelessly with her arms hanging down. Soelver laid his face close to hers. His breath was eager, his blood was on fire and in his fierce wrath he intended to yield himself to the boiling heat of sensual passion. Her cheeks however, her skin, her lips were cold as those of death. He began nevertheless wildly to kiss her face, once and again, as if to waken warmth and life in the cold skin. Yet with every kiss it was as if she grew more fixed, as if the lips shriveled and grew cold and damp as ice over the teeth. The cold from this embrace crept over Soelver, and drew the heat and fervor from his nerves, until he shook suddenly with the cold and shuddered with the thought that he had a corpse under him. Yet in that selfsame moment he marked the rising of her breast as she drew in her breath, full of strength with all its coldness, so full of strength that it pushed Soelver away and he slipped down to the hard flags of the floor.

"Soelver lay upon the floor, congealed with a coldness which was stronger than that of the hard tiles. It was as dark as in a walled-in grave. He dared not move however for fear that he would again feel that ice cold body. 'Hear me,' sounded suddenly a strangely shrill whisper, 'hear me, if you are a man, let me get out! Call my father! I want to get out--make light--give me air--I am almost choking--I want to get out!'" As Soelver opened the shutter again so that the dim shadowy glow of the night could enter, he saw Gro "tall and slender in the pale light." "Let me out, let me out!" she begged. "I am afraid here below--not of you--but of myself and of the dark--let me out!" "For the first time Soelver heard a soft rhythm in this voice smooth as steel. A soft breath breathed itself in her entreaty. He became a man, a protector and felt his power grow through her supplication."

Yet though he exerted himself to the utmost to open the door of his dungeon, it was all in vain. It must have been fastened on the outside with massive oak or iron bars. "So finally he gave up entirely and turned back to the opening where the light came in. Gro had sunk down under the last bit of light, without complaint, without sound. Her eyes were closed, she leaned her head against the sharp edge of the aperture and her arms hung down lifelessly. Soelver bent over her; her breath was almost inaudible, but irregular and did not suggest sleep. Like a thirsty plant she stretched herself out of the single airhole of the dungeon that she might seize the last drop of light before the darkness extinguished everything. Soelver divined that she could not be brought away from this aperture for light." He brought all the skins from the couch, spread them over her, pushed them under her body and "solicitously, with infinite carefulness he protected her from the damp floor, while he shoved his arm under her for support without ever touching her with his hand. All his brutality was gone, all his burning passion. Here she lay before him like a delicate sick flower, which must be covered over from the cold of night."

When Soelver awoke the next morning he noticed that one of his hands was seized by her, grasped in the unconsciousness of sleep and held fast by her long, slender fingers, which clasped themselves about his hand. It was as if her soul clung to him in sleep as helper and savior from him himself, from his own brutal savagery. When Gro however opened her eyes and stared into

Soelver's face, lit up by the sun, she broke out into weeping which could not be stilled. "She was terrified at awaking in a cellar hole, into the close damp darkness of which she looked, while the face of her vanquisher blazed strong in the sunlight before her; she wept without understanding or comprehending anything of what had happened about her." Perplexed, Soelver bent over her hand and kissed it. Then came Sten Basse and saw how uncontrollably Gro sobbed. "If you have gone near my daughter," he hissed at the young nobleman, "there will be no punishment strong enough for you." At this there shot up in Soelver a wild lust for revenge and he answered his enemy with irritating coldness: "Yes, I took what you gave. You brought her yourself into my presence, you laid her yourself in my arms. Now you may take her back again. I spurn your daughter for I have not desired her for the honor and keeping of my house, but only for the entertainment of a night. Take her back now! Take her back!"

Nevertheless better treatment was from this time on accorded Soelver, which he never for a moment doubted he owed to Gro. As he dwelt in his cell upon his phantasies, he suddenly heard her voice singing that melancholy song of Sir Tidemand, who tried to lure the maiden Blidelille into his boat by vigorous runes written upon roses. Blidelille awoke at midnight and knew not what it was that compelled her.

"It drew me along to Sir Tidemand Whom never mine eyes had seen."

In vain the foster mother bids them spread velvets and satins over her that she might sleep. Notwithstanding she arises suddenly, dresses herself and goes down to the strand to Sir Tidemand, who meets her scornfully. Then she goes into the lake, whither Tidemand follows her, seized with heartfelt remorse.

"For evil the rune on the rose leaf traced And evil the work it had wrought, That two so noble, of royal grace, To ruin and death were brought."

The woful song trailed itself through Soelver's mind like an indistinct dream. Then he believed that he distinguished Gro's step, until it was lost in her sleeping room. With his mental vision he saw the maiden, as she looked out upon the lake toward Aebeloe. She looked away from him, of whose fate she took no thought, but gazed fixedly over the sea, which bore upon its bosom a ship with silken sails, on whose deck Sir Tidemand stood. "Then Soelver was conscious of an infinite weakness in his love toward this pure maiden, whom his coarseness had taken into his arms, his desire had scorched with its hot breath but who had nevertheless left him benumbed in his baseness, cowardliness and weakness. Now he understood that love, in order to triumph, must first humble its own power, still its own movement and soften its brutal will. Now he comprehended that he must carve mystic runes of passion upon his own heart as upon a glowing rose and fling it into the mighty sea of feeling, praying it to bring the maiden Gro into his hands."

Day and night Soelver's thoughts tarried only with Gro. In his phantasies "he forced himself through the bolted door, climbed sharp angled passage ways and winding staircases and lifted oaken beams from barred doors. Without once making a mistake, driven by a magic sense of direction, he finally reached Gro's couch, at which he saw himself staring with great white eyes, whose pupils in the darkness of sleep had as it were glided over to the side. And upon the cover of her couch lay her two gleaming arms and the fingers of the right hand trembled as if they grasped another invisible hand. In this room Soelver remained until her sleep drew him to itself, until the heaving of her breasts drew him down, until her fingers entwined themselves with his, until their breath mingled and his lids closed before her pure gaze."

Another time he dreamed that he was upon a vessel, evidently in the role of Sir Tidemand. And Gro actually came over the water to him like the maiden Blidelille, "with roses like two blood spots upon her breast. She had crossed her hands beneath them and fastened her pure gaze upon Soelver, so that he was seized with terror and, without escaping her look, fled to the lee of the vessel to the edge of the ship. Yet Gro steadily drew nearer. Now she reached the ship's border and Soelver retreated. Step by step she followed him, the painful gaze of her deathly white face absorbed by his own. And he withdrew over to the other border, drew back until he felt the railing hard behind him. Gro stepped forward alone and it was not possible to stop her; he felt as if she wished to press within him like the sped arrow to its goal. Finally, in an instant, as her garment fluttered against him, he threw himself with a loud cry to one side and saw, with a great horror, that Gro went forward, through the railing as through air and disappeared on the other side in the sea, while Soelver lay moaning upon the deck and saw before him only the red roses, which fallen from her breast crept like living blood over the ship's planks."

Was it dream or reality, which he saw when he opened his eyes? "The sun's rays burst forth through a crack in a long, radiant arrow, which bored itself into the floor and transfixed as it were something red that began to glow." And as Soelver crept nearer his astonishment grew deeper. "For hard by the vision of red were footprints breathed so to speak upon the floor, fine, slender prints, directed toward him, no more distinct than if a warm breeze had blown away the dampness from the surface of a stone, leaving the outline of a foot fixed there." As he now stooped down and with his hand felt for the blood red spot, his fingers actually touched "a heavy full-blown rose, whose sweet strong odor he drank as if in an intoxication of reality." No one had forced his way in through the hatchway, of this he soon convinced himself. Gro must have dropped it here while he was spinning dreams about her.

In the nights which followed "he slept in a kind of hunger to feel her physically and tangibly in his arms." Then when it was again full moon, he found on awaking, in a spot upon which fell the rays of moonlight, a little gold cross, "whose six polished stones seemed to radiate moonlight from themselves. It was as if the moonlight lay within his hand. He watched the small cross sparkle--it was the same that he had seen in dreams upon her rose wreath. Gro had been also within his prison."

He was led out soon after this to be shown to the monk, who had come to obtain news of his imprisonment. "In the doorway the young nobleman met Gro and drew back, so strong a power seemed to irradiate from her living form. She stood in the half twilight, with her white hands and her white neck and forehead, which shone as with their own light from out her coal black velvet robe. There was a blinding, marvelous reality about her, which drew him like a great fragrant flower." As the monk expressed his compassion for him, that imprisonment had befallen him, his pride of nobility awoke. "What do you say of imprisonment and ill foreboding? Know you not then that I am of my free will Sten Basse's guest?" This reply astonished even Sten Basse. "He admired the young, undaunted spirit, who found in himself no occasion for pity. Soelver stood before Gro, his arms firm at his sides, and breathed deep and strong. His eyes drank in the clear light from her hands and face." When however Sten Basse sought to approach him in a friendly manner, Soelver motioned him back: "As prisoner was I led forth, as prisoner I return of my free will. If you wish to make any apology to me, you know where my dungeon is to be found." Then he went quickly, without turning toward Gro, out of the hall and down into his prison. His senses nevertheless had seized that warm, radiant picture of the beautiful Gro and transplanted it to the midst of his cell. He saw it streaming before his eyes in the shimmering light of the cross of moonlight and longed for the clear light of the night, that he might go on and make the dream face live. When the darkness advanced "he stripped himself naked and allowed the air of the summer night to cool his limbs and purify them, before he betook himself to his cot. The small cross he laid upon his naked breast and watched the moonlight glimmer green and blue from every stone" and kissed it thinking of Gro. Then he fell asleep in blissful happiness.

Suddenly however he awoke without any apparent reason, from no dream or thought. "He was awake, collected and yet at the same time strangely under the control of something that lay outside himself, a strange unknown power, which might be either mystical or natural. It appeared to him as if the moonlight had been loosed from the moon and now floated about in the room like a living being. So real seemed this fancy to him that he turned his head to one side and was not astonished actually to see a form standing in the center of the darkness. A feeling of reverence and awe swept over Soelver as little by little he distinguished in the floating folds of the moon white garment, the firm outlines of a woman's arms, which were crossed beneath a half bared breast, the line of the teeth in the open mouth, a flash of white light from Gro's eyes gazing with a certain fixed power.

"Holy Mother of God--it was Gro herself!

"Soelver started upright, frightened at his own movement, for he scarcely dared breathe, much less go towards her. He felt his nakedness as a crime, even his being awake as a transgression. The form glided forward out of the moonlight, the crossed hands separated themselves from the breast and Gro pursued her way with outstretched hands, feeling her way and yet mechanically sure like a sleep walker.

"Yes, she was walking in her sleep. Soelver recognized it by the staring look in her eyes, which gazed through the night as through miles of space. Soelver slid noiselessly to the floor in front of her, afraid that he would be seen, in deadly terror lest she should awaken. For he knew how dreadful it might be to awaken a sleep walker and in his excited phantasy he heard already the cry of horror and madness which would issue from Gro's mouth if she awoke and saw herself in this dark, subterranean depth alone with a naked man as with a demon. It was as if everything in Soelver cried out in protective anxiety that Gro should not awaken. He crouched beseechingly upon the ground, his whole soul was a sobbing prayer for grace, for instant means of deliverance, now that Gro had come to him as if by fate.

"There came a whispered sound from her open mouth, as her lips for a moment sought each other. It was as if she breathed out the one word 'Soelver.' This, however, to hear his name spoken, made Soelver strong at once. It compelled him to arise from the floor, it banished fear from his soul, it made him rejoice in every fiber of his being. The next moment her outstretched arm reached his hand--he felt the firm, cool skin under his trembling finger tips and his face felt the warm breathing of her voice, 'Soelver, Soelver!' And driven by some mystic power of will, he forced himself under the same hypnotic influence which surrounded her. He compelled himself to leave the clear broad way of reason and to enter the ecstatic, perilous, paths of the sleep walker. He was no longer awake. He sought, he touched, he stood before that after which he had groped. He was himself driven by a magic power, by a marvelous single purpose, which must be attained. This whole transformation took place in him merely because he felt that this was the only means of saving her from awaking to consciousness and madness.

"'Soelver--Soelver!'--'Yes.'--'Soelver--are you--are you--there?'--'Yes--I--am--here.'--'Yes--that is you--that is you--I feel you.'--'And you see me?'--'Yes, I see you.'--'And you will stay with me?'--'Yes--I will--I will stay with you.'

"Soelver answered her in the same whisperings in which she breathed out her words. His hands passed over hers with infinite carefulness. But finally his arms closed about her neck and he felt a marvelous tingling in his finger tips as he touched her soft silken hair. His mouth approached hers and mingled his warm breath with the breath which escaped cold from her lips. He drew in the air with her own rhythm, it was as if his naked heart bowed toward hers so that they all at once touched one another. Then the blood flamed out of her cheeks and streamed over into his, although they lay not upon each other.

The blood burned in all her skin and Soelver trembled for a moment lest this transport was the beginning of the awakening.

"His heart stood still with fear. However the blood continued to surge through Gro's body. She pressed Soelver close to herself and through her soft clothing he felt her breast swell and throb, as if she would bore herself into his flesh. 'Soelver--I love you.'--'Gro--I love you.' Then a strange giddiness seized him as if he were rushing into her arms on a tower miles high. He breathed upon her ethereal kisses, which closed her lips, moistened her forehead and descended thence like a refreshing spring rain so that her lids drooped. When her eyes were closed Soelver felt for the first time quite secure. He fastened them with a real kiss and now, since her sleep wandering had reached its goal in his arms and Soelver was sure that her love dream was too deep to be disturbed, he whispered louder than before, 'Gro--I love you!'--'Soelver--I love you!'--'How long have you loved me?'--'Longer than I have known you, Soelver.'--'Why have you not said so, Gro?'--'That, Soelver, I will never tell!'

"So Soelver carried his wonderful burden to his couch and inhaled her youthful fragrance and lifted his mouth to hers and all his blood at once leaped forth. Every fiber of his being was stirred to kisses, every blood drop became a yearning mouth to meet the thousand mouths of her blood. And lost to sense--vehemently, seized by the divine power of nature, unafraid that she might awaken, without control over himself and yet proud as a master of worlds, he was impelled as the sunbeam to its goal, when it forces open the flower and buries itself in its fragrant depths. Soelver united himself with Gro. She on her part slumbered on, quiet as the sea which has closed over its sacrifice.

"But Soelver felt his senses reawakening. What now? Should he let Gro sleep until day woke her and she saw herself in his arms? He bent over his beloved in deepest distress. She must not awaken in terror, not again weep as on that first morning when she was with him. The most delicate chords in her soul had trembled and sung to him in the night, to him whom she unconsciously loved with all the indefinable conviction of her heart. This love must not be rudely plucked and allowed to fade like a plant whose tender shoot is torn asunder. She must go back to her maiden's couch until the flower of the day had burst forth from its leafy covering. Then he discovered that the panel at the foot of his cot was opened, while some planking had been pushed back. Gro must have come this way and by this way he carried her back. Led by an unerring instinct, as if he knew from his nightly phantasied visits all the turnings of the way, he went without deliberation into the secret room behind the panel, found the passage to the main stairway, passed straight up, turned through corridors, passed under the heavy tapestry curtains, opened the last door and noticed first that he bore a burden when he laid it down. The moon threw its faint silver light round about in the little room. With a sweet wonder Soelver gazed upon the prayer stool and the brown rosary--without its cross."

I may pass briefly over the remainder. In the first place Soelver was given his liberty and he went back to his castle. The death of Sten Basse occurred soon after. Soelver whispered to his daughter at his death bed, "Gro, whatever may happen, know now that we belong to one another." She "turned her head slowly toward him and looked at him with her large eyes swollen with tears. Her look was that of a stranger and quite uncomprehending, so that Soelver understood that she did not simply deny everything but she had no recollection at all." So Soelver turned and went. For the first time when bathing in the lake "he found again his youth and his freedom, his radiant hope and the jubilant certainty of his love. Gro loved him! Only the thought of love had not yet arisen from the depths of her soul like pearls to the light. Nevertheless the wonderful flower of her affection was growing in the golden light of dreams. He longed after Gro as after his bride, although he was only the bridegroom of her dreams, who dared to kiss her only when her eyes were closed. By day he was her foe, as the bear in the fairy tale, who by night alone is changed into a beautiful young man."

They met therefore first again at Sten's bier, at the side of which they both kneeled. "Gro's eyes were directed upon him as upon a stranger, staring with wonder, burning with a mystic light. Why was this stranger here near her, the man whom her dead father had tortured and derided? And yet her eyes were wet with tears of pity and she felt that this man only desired to take her hand. Soelver observed her with his inmost soul. He pressed the small cross of moonshine between his hands, he bent over it and kissed it and a gleam from its blazing stones smote Gro's eyes. She stretched out her arms and took the cross from him and gazed into the stones as into well-known eyes. She knew not how this had come into Soelver's hands but she also bent over it and kissed it and her soul went out toward Soelver as toward a soul far, far away, whom she once had known, whom however she could scarcely remember."

After this Soelver came and went at Egenaes, Sten Basse's castle, as if he were lord and heir of the estate. "It was rumored also among the tenants and the servants that he was betrothed to the maiden Gro. Yet no word of it was exchanged between them. Soelver stood by Gro in small things and great, and she allowed herself to be guided by his strength and cleverness. Since that night when he had kneeled with her at her father's lifeless body, she was bound to him by a nameless bond of gratitude, of mutual feeling, and by an inner apprehension that their fate was interwoven. Still no consciousness of love colored Gro's attitude. She longed for Soelver's strong handclasp because it made her will strong to withstand her sorrow. She could think of herself lying upon his broad, deep breast, only however because there slumber would come in sure forgetfulness. There was moreover a tenderness in her look, when in a fleeting moment she let her glance rest upon his, such as the realization of another's goodness awakens in us, especially when the goodness is undeserved and disinterested. Yet there was never any of love's surrender. Only she was glad to know herself observed by these quiet, steadfast, clear eyes, from which the red specter of passion, which had so frightened her that day upon Aebeloe, had long been banished. She believed that she had in Soelver a friend given her for life and death, a friend who could not desire her in love nor be desired, a brother whom one might trust with infinitely more serenity than any lover.

"Soelver was ever watchful of Gro. His eyes were on the lookout whether he might not once surprise in hers the brightness of the dream, and make the hidden rose of love break through the green covering and bloom in reality. He longed thus within himself once to see the day and night aspects of her soul melt into a wonderful golden twilight. But Gro made no response to the gaze from his eyes. She turned her head aside so that her silken lashes concealed her glance. 'Gro, why do you never look at me?'--'I do look at you.'--'Do you see me with your cheek, Gro?'--'I see you, though, Soelver. I see you with the outermost corner of my eye.' Soelver bent his face beneath hers. 'Are you looking at me?' But Gro pressed her lids together as before a bright light and shook her head, 'No, Soelver, not so! You look too sharply, you look too deeply. You look so deeply that it hurts me very much. No, stand so Soelver, turn your eyes away!'--'Are you afraid of me?'--'No, no--why should I be afraid? But I do not feel comfortable to have you all the time wanting to read my heart, to have your eyes searching for some writing that does not stand written there. My friend and beloved brother, I fear what your look would draw from me--what would you drag out from my soul?'--'The spring day, Gro, when we first met.'--'Ah! Soelver, I scarcely remember it. It seems to me that I have always known you, that all your days you have been good and kind to me. Lately I have felt it in my heart and upon my cheek, as when my mother caressed me and that is long, long ago.'--'Gro, only say it, you are afraid of the word, but not truly--just say it--you love me.--You are silent because it is true.' 'No, Soelver, I have never felt that.'--'So you have dreamed it, Gro.'--'Dreamed!' Gro became fiery red. 'Dreamed--dreamed--oh Soelver, what have I dreamed? What do you know of my dreams? To have dreamed is to have dreamed, and my dreams belong to me, to me alone!' For a moment she turned to him a shy, quivering look, then tears trickled down from under her drooping lids. But Soelver observed that he had hit upon the truth. Immediately however he regretted that he had cast this look into the sanctuary of her soul. It was like the curious peeping of which the knight had been guilty, spying through the keyhole upon his wife, Undine.

"A long time they sat silent. At last Gro was herself again, quiet and controlled. Then she spoke in a soft but firm voice, 'Soelver, if you remain with me to awaken me to love, then I beg of you, go and never return. I can never look upon you with the eyes of love. Passion seems to me like a glowing sword, which burns out one's eyes as it goes by. There was a day when you made the flaming sword of your desire pass by my face--since that time it is burned out. I have been blinded, Soelver, I am blind to the desire of your eyes, and all your fervent prayers. I have hated you, despised you, defied you, yet you have repaid evil with good and now I return good for good. Look not upon me with love's eyes, seek not to awaken the dead in me to life. You are to me more precious than if the proud brother of my childhood had returned in you, your spirit is his, I did not believe that in the will of a man so much kindness could dwell. Leave it so, stay with me as my brother, or leave me like my brother, but never speak to me of love, neither in words nor in looks for I know no reply.'"

The young nobleman knew finally, for all his eager power, no other way of escape than to go with the king to the war. He saw quite clearly that "Gro struggled against the force deep in her heart. And yet the day's flaming sun could cause the weak chrysalis of the dream to shrivel so that no butterfly would break through the covering and rejoice in the strong light of midday. But with Soelver away, the longing for him would support the invisible growth of the dream and prepare the way for it into consciousness. Ah! it was worth his departure." Then he took leave of his beloved. "Goodbye; forget me not on our island. Bid me return when you will. The wind will find me, wherever I am. Tell the wild birds, when you want me and would call me home."

Gro, remaining behind alone, first became aware what she had lost in him and in his "strong will, which was her source of light." She began to long more and more for him who was far away. "Ah, if he would only come again!" And when a bird flew by, she "flushed red at her own thought; was that a message sent forth by her desire? This took place contrary to her wish and will--she wished not to long for him, not to call him back, not to love him! Angrily she roused herself and sought to recall the burning gaze with which Soelver had wounded her modesty. So with a vexed and hard stroke of the oars she pushed the boat away from Aebeloe."

When the war was ended, Soelver went to serve the king of France. For, as he wrote in a letter sent by carrier pigeon, "he who is not summoned, comes not." Meanwhile love towards the young nobleman had begun to grow in her bosom. "Night after night she dreamed of Soelver and at last one night she suddenly awoke and found herself cold and naked, wandering around in her room and heard the last note of her heart's unconscious avowal, 'Soelver, I love you.' There was a change within her. Hour after hour would she sit inactive and half asleep, listening to the irregular beating of her heart-- something was drawing upon her very depths, sucking her strength from her, from her proud will, something that paralyzed her thought and bound her always to the same name, the same memory." As she listened to her own depths, "she caught a momentary something like a weak, quickly beating echo of her own slow heart, a busily living little heart, that ticked louder and louder until at last it deafened hers. A trembling joy seized her at that moment through all her senses as she knew that she bore a life within her life, that she enclosed in her body the germ of a new life that was not growing from her alone and of her life alone."

Suddenly a crushing terror overcame her. Who was her child's father? "So abruptly came this question over her na 咫 e soul that she fancied for a moment that this might be the punishment of fate for her longing for Soelver. This longing was desire, and desire was sin no less than the love itself. Her wish for him had grown to a fire in her blood and now she was stained by her own passion, pregnant from her own sin. God's punishment had visited her and soon would be visible to all the world. Gro saw however immediately the foolishness of her thought. For one moment she lingered at the thought of the one woman of all the earth, who had immaculately conceived. Then she uttered an inward prayer that the Mother of God would lighten her understanding and give her clearness of vision that she should not go astray in her brooding over this mystery."

When she questioned her nurse and the latter finally put it to her, "Have you spent no night under the same roof with Soelver?" then there occurred to her the many nights "when she had dreamed of the lonely imprisoned man, who was being punished because of her. When she lay in her bed in the dark, a strange curiosity had overcome her to imagine his lot there below and, when sleep seized her and dreams chased away the bitter, hard thoughts, her heart had become softer and the sun had shone over the visions of her dreams as the spring day over the woods blossoming with the green May bells. Many a night and many a morning was she awakened by a strange burning desire in her thoughts, and her mouth was as though touched with fresh dream kisses, and she had entered into judgment with her own weak heart and had so inflamed herself to scorn and hatred that she had done nothing to soften the fate of the prisoner. But how could Soelver have been the guest of her dreams? And how had he been able to command the virgin love fed by her slumber? Then came the nurse to her aid and made it clear to her. She knew that the maiden Gro had walked in her sleep; the servants had told of a white ghost on the stairs and once she herself had seen it and recognized Gro, who had disappeared upon a secret stairway, which led down into the dungeon. She had kept still about it, for she thought it was a voluntary sleep walking to the young nobleman."

Thus was Gro enlightened as to the source of her pregnancy. "She quivered with shame that the desire in her dreams had the power to drive her down to the lonely prisoner and she shook in her inmost soul at the memory of that happy dream, which she had had the night before her father's death. Now her love suddenly burst into the light like a wonderful flower, which suddenly springs up with a thousand fragrant buds. Now it was impossible to stem it or to conceal it. She had wanted to suppress every germ, with her father's coldness and the day's dispassionately proud haughtiness she had been willing to stifle every impulse toward love, every longing for self avowal. Now she found her pride was dead and buried and her being within and without was permeated by love.

"For she had loved Soelver from the first springtime kiss, which he had imprinted upon her cheek as she wandered among the fresh May bells, loved him in the blow which she had inflicted upon his head when he had touched her chaste nakedness, loved him in those nights when he had slept uncomplaining in the cellar dungeon, loved him in those bitter moments of his humbling when he, in spite of scorn and insult, maintained his pride, loved him that evening when he kneeled at her father's bier and kissed the hand of his enemy now dead, loved him day by day all the time they were together, loved him in that hour when she saw his banner disappear among the hundred others, and today upon Aebeloe when she heard that new life singing within hers. And now she rejoiced; for she bore him always within her, she could never again lose her Soelver."

As we glance over the material of this tale, we find as the nucleus of the night wandering and moon walking the strong repression of every conscious love impulse and the breaking through of the unconscious in sleep and dream wherever the censor's rule is relaxed. For the maiden Gro had loved Soelver from the first moment, yet this love was confessed only in moments of occasional self forgetfulness, as by the first meeting with the young nobleman, when her hand met his, yes, even pressed it for the moment. Only Gro should not have been frightened out of her half unconscious action by a kiss or a passionate desire, for at once there arose to life within her the coldness and haughtiness of her father and the highhanded reaction which her mother had manifested to her conqueror. The determining factor, to speak in psychoanalytic language, is the struggle between the strong sexual rejection and the equally compelling sexual desire. At first the former held the upper hand with our heroine in her waking and conscious action, the latter in the unconscious. Through the force of her will Gro seemed cold, even as she had learned of her father. She defended herself from her lover's craving by force and blow; even when conquered finally through the noble spirit of her enemy, she would see in him only the friend for life and death. She directly refused to think of love and displaced it to external things, she even bade the young man go rather than desire her as his wife. Soelver's devotion reminded her most significantly of her mother's tenderness, his pride, of the brother of her childhood. "It is as if in you the proud brother of my childhood had returned. Your spirit is his. Leave it so, stay with me as my brother or leave me like my brother, but never speak to me of love, neither in words nor in looks, for I know no reply!"

Yet she avoided Soelver's searching eye and as he reminded her of her dreams, she was smitten in the depths of her soul. For her dreams, she well knew, chased away the bitter and hard thoughts, the repressed unconscious broke through and the true feeling of her loving heart. This already appeared clear to her when her beloved languished in captivity at her father's hands. The strange desire to work out the fate of the young nobleman, who suffered on her account, had overcome her lying there in her bed in the dark. And in the morning she awoke with a strange burning desire in her thoughts and her mouth was flecked with his fresh dream kisses. Still she consciously kept back every outer manifestation of love and met the young man while her father was alive with coldness and suspicion and later even merely as a brother. The great distance separating her beloved from her and above all the child which she bore from him under her heart for the first time conquer her haughty pride and her conscious aversion. And as she dreams one night again of the loved one far away she finds herself suddenly awake, going about cold and naked in her room and perceives as the lingering sound of her heart's unconscious avowal, "Soelver, I love you!"

So severe is this struggle between conscious sexual denial and unconscious desire, that it even forces itself through in her sleep and her night wandering. Her dreams had indeed, as she later acknowledged with shame, the force and the power to compel her below into the young nobleman's dungeon. She had clasped Soelver's hand in her sleep, she had told him everything in the moonlight, with eyes closed, everything which she secretly felt, and had pressed him to herself. Yet when he asked her why she could never confess to him that she had always loved him so deeply, she repulsed him: "That I will never tell!" Even when he had united himself to his beloved, she had slumbered on as if nothing had happened and the next day knew nothing of it all.

This leads now to that which, according to folk belief, constitutes the very core, the chief ground for sleep walking and moon walking in a maiden. It is easy to understand the wish, on the part of the female sex with their strongly demanded sexual repression, to come to the beloved one and taste all the delights of satisfaction but without guilt. This is possible only through wandering in unconscious sleep. For, as my first patient explained, one is not accountable for anything that happens in this state, and thus can enjoy without sin and without consciousness of what is not permitted. Convention demands that the maiden wait until the lover approaches her, but in that unconscious state she may surrender herself. The need for repression explains then the subsequent amnesia. Yet wandering by night is not concerned merely with sexual enjoyment, over and above that it fulfills a second desire that arises out of childhood, as we know from psychoanalysis. Every small maiden has, that is, the wish to have a child by her father, her first love, which is often in later years defined thus, one might have a child, but without a husband. The night wandering fulfills this desire to have a child yet without sin. Therefore has that motive of an unconscious, not to say immaculate, conception inspired not a few poets, as it has already, as is well known, been active in the creation of the drama.

Less transparent than that chief motive is the action of the light, sunlight as well as moonlight. The heroine of the story stands toward both in a special relationship. Her body is almost illuminated by its own light, her hair sparkles electrically when it is touched, "warm waves of light" emanate from her, which Soelver noticed at their first meeting, the sun seems expressly to seek her, a halo of impalpable beauty surrounds her and above all glows from the depths of her eyes. Not only so, Gro seems to dwell chiefly in the light, whose last drops she greedily absorbs within herself. When the light fades, her body becomes cold as ice like a corpse. In similar manner the shining of the full moon affects her, the light of which the stones of her gold cross have absorbed. The first time that the slumbering youth saw Gro wandering, it seemed to him as if the moonlight had been loosed from the planet and floated only in his room like a living being. The poet, to be sure, has offered no explanation of this mystical effect of light and what the reader may think for himself would be merely drawn from other sources. For this reason I will not pursue this point further.

The narrative affords somewhat further means for an understanding in another direction. It is not explained more fully just why Gro follows the sunlight and moonlight or why both exercise upon her a peculiar attraction, yet the tendency to a motor breaking through of the unconscious may be derived from an inherited disposition. The father is a rough, violent robber knight while the mother shows distinctly sadistic traits and a truly ready hand at fighting. That confirms what I explained in the first part, a heightened muscular excitability and muscle eroticism, which strives to break through again on the sexual side in sleep walking. Finally it may be affirmed without doubt that the ghostly white figure upon the stairs was no other than the maiden in her shift.

"J 諶 N UHL," by Gustav Frenssen.

I can deal more briefly with "J 鍵 n Uhl," the well-known rural romance of Frenssen, in which the sketch of a moon walker constitutes merely an episode. Joern Uhl, who, returned from the war, takes over the farm of his unfortunate father, discovers Lena Tarn as the head maid-servant. She pleased him at first sight. "She was large and strong and stately in her walk. Besides her face was fresh with color, white and red, her hair golden and slightly wavy. He thought he had never seen so fresh and at the same time so goodly appearing a girl. He was pleased also at the way she nodded to him and said 'good evening' and looked him over from head to foot with such open curiosity and sincere friendliness." She sings too much to please the old housekeeper! "She is so pert and too straightforward with her speech." It is noteworthy too that she talks to herself in unquiet sleep.

Lena Tarn can soon make observations also upon her side. Joern was very short with the old graybeard, who advised him to an early marriage: "The housekeeper is with me, I do not need a wife." Lena, entering just then, heard what the unmannerly countryman said and assumed a proud look, thinking to herself, "What is the sly old man saying!" Since however the old man began to talk and compelled her and Joern Uhl to listen, she was concerned almost entirely for the latter, whose "long, quiet face with its deep discerning eyes she observed with a silent wonder, without shyness, but with confident curiosity." Not alone in the kitchen, which is under her control, can Lena show what is in her. When a young bull broke loose and came after the women, she met him with sparkling eyes, "Stop you wretch!" When he would not allow himself to be turned aside, she threw a swift look flashing with anger upon the men, who were idly looking on, then swung the three-legged milking stool which she had taken along and hit the bull so forcibly on the head with it that frightened, he lunged off sideways. "Lena Tarn had however all afternoon a red glow coming and going in her cheeks because the farmer had looked upon her with the eyes of a high and mighty young man. That caused her secretly both joy and concern." Immediately after this she experienced one satisfaction. Joern Uhl was dragged into the water by a mischievous calf and was much worse cut up by it than she, the weaker one, the woman had been.

"Lena saw always before her the face which Joern Uhl had made when she had gone forward against the bull. She was otherwise in the best of humors, but when, as in the last few days, she was not quite well physically she was inclined to be angry. She preserved a gloomy countenance as well and as long as she could. Soon though, as she went here and there about her work and felt the new fresh health streaming through her limbs, she altered her looks.... Joern Uhl moreover could not be quiet that day. The sudden plunge in the water had brought his blood to boiling. The spring sunshine did its part. A holiday spirit came over him and he thought that he would go into the village and pay his taxes, which were due. On the way he thought of Lena Tarn. Her hair is coiled upon her head like a helmet of burnished brass, which slips into her neck. When she 'does things,' as she says, her eyes are stern and directed eagerly upon her work. When on the other hand she is spoken to and speaks with any one she is quick to laugh. Work seems to her the only field where quiet earnestness is in place. 'That must be so,' she says. Toward everything else she is angry or in a good humor, mostly the latter. Only toward me is she short and often spiteful. It has been a great joke for her that I had the ill luck to have to go into the water with that stupid beast. If she only dared she would spread it three times a day on my bread and butter and say 'There you have it.'"

Now he meets old Dreier who gives him good advice: "How old are you? Twenty-four? Don't you marry, Joern. On no account. That would be the stupidest thing that you could do. I bet you $50.000 you don't dare do it. Time will tell, I say." "Take it for granted that I will wait yet ten years," he answered. And he went on thinking to himself, "It is pleasanter to go thus alone and let one's thoughts run on. Marry? Marry now? I will be on my guard. After I am thirty!" Then his thought came back to Lena. "She looked well as she flung the stool at the bull. Prancing like a three-year-old horse.

Yesterday she did not look so well, her eyes were not so bright, she spoke harshly to Wieten (the old housekeeper) and said to her afterwards, 'Do not mind it, Wieten, I slept badly,' and laughed. Funny thing, slept badly? When one is on the go as she must be all day, one should sleep like a log. But that is all right in the May days. It is well that men understand this, otherwise every spring the world would go all to pieces." Then he rejoiced that he was so young and could point out on the farm what was his. "Later, when the years have gone by and I am well established I will take to myself a fine wife with money and golden hair. There are also rich girls who are as merry and fresh and as desirable and have as stately forms. It need not be just this one."

Then he came to the parish clerk who had just been notified that day of six children to be baptized and who was complaining of the increase in births. Joern agreed with him: "What will we come to, if the folk increase like that? Marrying before twenty-five must simply be forbidden." "With these words he departed, filled with a proud consciousness that he was of the same opinion with so intelligent, experienced an old man as the parish clerk." At home he met Lena Tarn with an old farmer, who came to inquire after the fate of his son who had been with Joern in the war. Then for the first time the girl heard of the frightful misery and the suffering of the soldiers which cried to heaven, so that her face was drawn with pain. "Deep in her soul however thrilled and laughed a secret joy, that you have come back whole, Joern Uhl."

Later, when she was making out the butter account with the farmer, "she had to bend her glowing head over the book, which he held in his hand. There came such a glistening in his eyes that he wrinkled his forehead and did not conceal his displeasure at such an unsteady flashing." In the evening she came to get back the book. Then Joern spoke to her, "You have not been in a good humor these last days. Is anything the matter?" She threw her head back and said shortly, "Something is the matter sometimes with one; but it soon passes over."--"As I came through the passage yesterday evening I heard you call out in your sleep in your room." "Oh, well!... I have not been well."--"What ... you not well? The moon has done that. It has been shining into your room."--"I say, though, there may be some other cause for that."--"I say that comes from the moon." She looked at him angrily, "As if you knew everything! I did not call out in my sleep at all but was wide awake. Three calves had broken out and were frisking around in the grass. I saw them clearly in the moonlight. I called them." He laughed mockingly, "Those certainly were moon calves." "So? I believe not. For I brought them in myself this morning and then I saw that the stable door stood open. I thought to myself, the boy has gone courting tonight. Your eyes always sweep over everything and light upon everything and you [du] worry so over everything out of order, I wonder that you [du] have not seen it."--"You say 'thou' [du] to me?"--"Yes, you say it to me. I am almost as great as you and you are not a count, and I am as intelligent as you." She carried her head pretty high and as she snatched the book from the window seat as if it lay there in the fire, he saw the splendid scorn in her eyes. "Take care of yourself when the moon is shining," he said, "otherwise again tonight you will have to guard the calves."

"He had arisen, but dared not touch her. They looked at one another however and each knew how it stood with the other. He had again the look which he had revealed once in the morning, a presuming look, confident of victory, such a look as if he would say, 'I know well enough how such a maidenly scorn is to be interpreted.' But her eyes said, 'I am too proud to love you.' She went slowly into the darkness of her room as if she would give him time yet to say something or to long after her. He was however too slow for that and laughed in confusion."

The night fell upon them, a wonderful still night. "I will take one more look at the moon," thought Joern Uhl and took his telescope. He went through the middle door with as little noise as possible, but the door of Lena's room stood open and she appeared upon the threshold and leaned against the side post. "Are you still awake?" he asked anxiously. "It is not yet late."--"The sky is so clear. I want to look at the stars once more. If you wish you may come with me." At first she remained standing, then he heard her coming after him. When he had directed his telescope to a nebulous star he invited her to look in. She placed herself so awkwardly that he laid his hand on her shoulder and asked her, "What do you see?"--"Oh!" she said, "I see--I see--a large farmhouse, which is burning. It has a thatched roof. Oh!--Everything is burning; the roof is all in flames. Sparks are flying about. It is really an old Ditmarsh farmhouse."--"No, my girl, you have too much imagination, which is bad for science.--What else do you see?"--"I see--I see--at one side of the farmhouse a plank which is dark; for the burning house is behind it. But I can look deep into the burning hall. Three, four sheaves have fallen from the loft and lie burning on the blazing floor. Oh, how frightful that is! Show me another house which is not burning.--Show me a house, you know, show me a farmyard just where they are who hunt up the calves." He laughed merrily. "You huzzy," said he, "you might well see your three-legged stool in the sky, not? So, high overhead!"--"You should have had the three-legged stool. I do not forget you that day, you ... and how you looked at me. That you may believe."

He had never yet let anyone share in his observations. Now he marveled and was pleased at her astonishment and joy. And then he showed her the moon. He placed her and held her again by the arm as if she were an awkward child. She was astonished at the masses on it: "What are those? Boiling things, like in our copper kettles? Exactly. What if it hung brightly scoured over our fireplace and tomorrow morning the fire shone up upon it."--"The boiling things are mountains and valleys.--And now you have seen enough and spoken wisely enough. Go inside. You will be cold and then you will dream again and see in the dream I do not know what. Will you be able to sleep?"--"I will try." He wanted again to reach out his hand to her but his high respect for her held him back. He thought he should not grasp her thus, along the way as it were. "Make haste," he said, "to get away."

She went and he remained to pursue his studies. So the time passed. He had grown eager and busied himself noiselessly with his telescope. "And he thrust aside once more that young life, which an hour ago had breathed so very near him and came again to the old beaten track of thought that the old Dreier was right. 'Don't do anything foolish, Joern.'--And yet, 'Fine she is and good. Happy the man about whose neck her arms lie.--What precious treasure must those eyes hold, when they can look with such frank confidence at a man.'"

About him now were only the customary sounds of night. Suddenly it was as if near by over the house roof and then at the side at the wall of the house he heard the soft cry of a goose and the weak flapping of wings. And "as he looked, there stood under the house roof in the bright moonlight a white human form, with one hand over the eyes and with the other feeling along the wall, as if it would enter the house where there was however no door. It spoke in excited hurried words, 'The calves are in the garden; you must be more on the watch. Get up Joern and help me.' Joern Uhl came in three long strides over the turf and softly called her name: 'I am here.--Here I stand.--It is I.--So! so!--Now be still.--It is I.--No one else is here.' She was speechless and began to rub her eyes with the back of her hand, as a child rubs the sleep out of its eyes, and she fretted also in childish fashion. Then he embraced her and told her again where she was, and led her to the stable door seeking to comfort her. 'Look, here is the door of the stable. Here you have gone through, you dreamer; you have gone all through the stable in your sleep. Have you been seeking the moon calves? Ah you foolish child!--So, here you need not be anxious. You will straightway be back in your room.' When she finally clearly recognized her situation, she was frightened, flung her hands against her face and uttered mournful cries. 'Oh, oh, how frightful this is!' But he caressed her, took her hands from her face and said to her feelingly, 'Now stop that complaining. Let it be as it is.' So they came to the open door, which led to her room. It must have been a remarkable night, for not only had half the calves in the pasture broken out and in the morning were actually standing in the garden and the court, but the boy this night of all nights had not come home, but only returned in the early morning twilight."

The next morning Joern Uhl went to the parish clerk that the banns might be published for him and the nineteen year old Lena Tarn. He was almost embarrassed when he came again before her, "I should merely like to know what you think of me." As she remained speechless, he came nearer. "You have always been a great heroine, especially to me. Hold your head high and make it known that I am right." She was still silent, merely pressed both hands to her temples and stared into the glowing hearth. Then he drew one of her hands down softly from her hair, seized it and went with her over the vestibule, through the door communicating with the front of the house. She followed him passively, her eyes upon the ground and the other hand still on her hair. In the living room he led her to the large chair which stood by the window and forced her into it. "So," said he softly, "here we are all alone, Lena. Here in this chair has Mother sat many a Sunday afternoon. You now belong in it." Still she said nothing. "I have been to the parish clerk and arranged everything and the wedding will be in June. Have you nothing to say yet?" Then she seized his hands and said softly, "As you think, it is all good so." And she covered her face with her hands and wept. Then he began to stroke her and kiss her. "Child, only cease your weeping. You are my fair little bride. Only be happy again." And in his distress he said, "I will never do it again. Only laugh again." At last when he could think of no more cajoling names, he called her "Redhead." Then she had to laugh, for that was the name of the best cow, which stood first in the stalls. Now she lifted her head and gazed long at him without moving. Thus Joern Uhl came rightly to that tenderness and comfort which he thought he deserved.

I have only a little to add that is important for our theme. As a young wife also Lena Tarn was busy the whole day, working from early to late without rest. The work flew from her hand. And when her confinement was over, she got up the sixth day, against the earnest warning of the housekeeper, cared for her boy alone the whole day, went even to the kitchen and carried water for his bath. Joern Uhl allowed it. For he was proud to have such a strong wife, "not so affected as the others." It led however to her death. Somehow she must have become infected, for soon after a severe childbed fever broke out.

Even as a young wife she, the poor humble cottager's daughter whose childhood was pinched by bitterest need, shed a wealth of love and joy upon all who dwelt about her. Yet now, "she, the friendly one, who had never caused suffering to any one, went in her fever delirium to every one in the house, even the smallest servant boy and to every neighbor and begged their forgiveness, 'if I have done anything to hurt you in any way.' Towards morning she became quieter but it was the exhaustion of death and she spoke with great difficulty. Her husband must 'tell Father that she had loved him.' Joern Uhl sobbed violently: 'Who has never spoken a kind word to you, poor child.' She tried to smile. 'You have had nothing but toil and work,' he said. Then she made him understand in labored speech that she had been very happy." The last fever phantasies finally put her back into her childhood. Her love went out to the old teacher Karstensen, then again to Joern Uhl, until she was finally led through angels to a further father-incarnation, to the dear God. "It came to her like peace and strength. Clasped by many hands and led forward, she came to an earnest, holy form who leaned forward and looked kindly upon her. Then she stretched her hand out and suddenly she had a great bunch of glowing red flowers in her hand. She gave them to him saying, 'That is all that I have. I pray you let me remain with you. I am fearfully weary. Afterwards I will work as hard as I can. If you would like to hear it, I will gladly sing at my work.'"

Scarcely in any other tale is the fierce strife between the clearly active sexual longing, and the conscious sexual denial present at the same time, as well as the final victory which the unconscious attains, so plainly shown as in Gustav Frenssen's romance, where the moon walking, exhibitionistic woman completely overthrows the reasoning of the man. The poet expresses it clearly and decisively: They each knew the desire of the other. Joern Uhl saw through the meaning of a maiden's scorn and Lena's eyes said, I am too proud to love you, but I do love you. Yet opportunity must be given to the unconscious to break through victoriously so that the inhibiting reason shall be deprived of its power. Therefore the powerful increase of libido with the woman during the occurrence of menstruation and through the wooing of the boy, who lets the calves break out, in the man through the cold bath and furthermore in both through the seductive May air. Finally the moon acts directly with its light as a precipitating cause.

The night before she had spoken out loud in her sleep just as Joern Uhl went by to his room. He had spoken of it directly as the action of the moonlight, which she of course contradicted; she had been lying awake and heard the calves break out.[19] Then she takes the following night, when the housekeeper, with whom she slept, was sitting up nursing an old farmer and the boy had gone courting again, to approach Joern Uhl on her part as a moon walker, who knew nothing of what she did and could not be held responsible. More than this her unconscious had a fitting speech ready, the calves had broken out again.

[19] Has not the bringing in of these animals and of the word mooncalves a hidden closeness of meaning? The repetition twice of the same motive, the analogy with the case at the beginning which I analyzed, and at last the fact that Lena, when she looked at the stars, wanted to see a farmhouse where some one was just driving out the calves, all this gives food for thought.

The breaking through of the motor impulse is also well grounded. Everything with Lena Tarn is joy in muscular activity, the restless, almost unappeasable desire for work and pleasurable "getting things done," "exerting herself," the constant singing, the easy giving way to anger. Work is the only thing which she can carry on earnestly because in that she lives out in part her sexuality, she meets every one else smilingly or angrily according to her mood. It is noteworthy too that her unquiet libido transforms itself toward Joern Uhl into anger and animosity and so much so that once in anger she addresses him as "thou" and acts as if she were his beloved.

One thing is especially evident in this example of sleep walking and moon walking, the invariably infantile bearing of these phenomena. When Lena, walking in her sleep, was called by her lover, she rubbed her eyes with the back of her hand as a child rubs the sleep from its eyelids and fretted also in childish fashion. Then again there is her strange behavior when Joern announces that he has arranged for the publishing of the banns. The farmer had in a significant way put her literally into the mother's place and then in the same manner shown tenderness toward her, stroking and caressing her, as he himself had once been treated by his mother. Still Lena, who already in the night responded to the sudden realization of her position with the cry, "Oh, oh, how frightful this is!" cannot yet quiet herself. It is hardly to be believed that a farm maiden would so lose control of herself at the thought of an illegitimate relationship, which furthermore was to be immediately legalized by marriage. Many things however point to this--I mention only her later fever phantasies--that she always felt inwardly guilty because she had been untrue to some one else, the first beloved of her childhood, her own father. Only when Joern Uhl on his part becomes a child and in his way solemnly declares, "I will never do it again," and in the end names her "Redhead," apparently a pet name of her parent, then she has to laugh and looks long at him without moving, wondering perhaps if he is the real father. After this everything falls into proper place. I can now somewhat extend the statement at the beginning of this section. Night wandering and moon walking have not only inner connections with the infantile but more exactly with the infantile erotic.

I will briefly mention still one circumstance in conclusion. The influence of the moonlight is but little touched upon in our tale. Joern Uhl speaks of it only once. There is on the contrary a connection with actual occurrences, a recent cause for Lena's moon walking. She has looked at the moon through the lover's telescope and received instruction in regard to it. That wakens the memory of the instruction of the old Karstensen, her teacher when she attended the folk school, from which we understand that he appears in the place of her father.

"MARIA," by Otto Ludwig.

Perhaps no poet has felt so deeply and expressed so clearly what constitutes the fundamental problem of sleep walking and moon walking as Otto Ludwig in his youthful novel "Maria." This novel has, according to a letter from the poet, "sprung from the anecdote of the rich young linen draper, who was passionately roused to commit an unnatural offence at sight of the landlord's daughter laid out apparently dead in the room through which he was conducted to his own. As a result of this, when he put up there years after, he found her, whom he supposed to have been buried, a mother, who had no knowledge as to who was her child's father."

This anecdote, which he learned from a friend, took such a hold upon him that he immediately wrote down not only what he had heard but the first plan, although upon the insistent protestation of that friend he did not work out the story as it had been first conceived nor so glaringly. "I saw," writes our poet, "at first only the psychological interest in this material. The problem was to present the story as well as possible and this was indeed a significant one for the narrator. A distinctly esthetic interest would not be possible in conjunction with that."

There is no doubt in the mind of the experienced psychoanalyst that, when a poet is laid hold of in this manner by an anecdote, this only happens because his own significant infantile complexes are roused out of the unconscious. Also the transformations, not unworthy of consideration, which the poet makes with the story are highly indicative. The seemingly dead maiden becomes a moon walker, the landlord's daughter is changed to the attractive daughter of a pastor. "Out of the linen draper there is finally made a cultivated, artistically sensitive youth, who has in him much of Ludwig's own personality" (Borcherdt). The finished romance the poet considered the best which he had so far created, it came nearest to his ideal of a story. Although his attempts always failed to find a publisher for the "Maria," the poet retained his love for this work all his life and it was one of the few productions of his youth which he occasionally still shared with his friends in his last years.

The theme of "Maria" is, as indeed the significant title represents, the unconscious, not to say, the immaculate conception. It is unconscious because the heroine, drawn by the moon and walking in her sleep, comes to her beloved and becomes pregnant by him without a conscious memory of the experience. Furthermore the analogy with the Mother of God becomes emphasized by the fact that in a picture "Mary and Magdalene" described at the beginning, the Queen of Heaven bears quite unmistakably the features of the heroine of the title. The main event, with its results and discovery, is developed out of the character of both hero and heroine with extraordinary psychical keenness.

Eisener like Maria is the only child of rich parents. For both love manifests itself for the most part rather unfortunately. Apparently neither gets on well with the father and both have early lost their mothers. Only Eisener even yet clings with deepest veneration to the mother who taught him to revere all women and, judging from his words, her influence upon her husband and the son's desire still appears. "Whatever of good there is in me, I owe to women. The thought of my excellent mother restrained me from many an indiscretion, as also the teaching and the example of the wisest and best of men (the father). This gentle power which is so sweet to obey and at the same time so full of reward! In loving surrender it obeys the man, while its divine power rules the man without his knowing it. The imperceptible but mighty influence of her gentle presence has determined his decision before he has comprehended it. It has fallen upon him in his anger like an angel before his own strength could arm itself, it has turned him to what is right and proper before he is conscious of the choice. Before her clear look confusion cannot exist, the coarse word of insolence sinks back unspoken into the shame filled breast. The brightness of a lost paradise shines from her eyes upon the fallen bringing pain and warning, the consolation of eternal pity smiles upon the penitent. These are the suns about which the planets of greatness, honor and beauty revolve, lighted and warmed by them." Maria's mother on the other hand is not praised by a single syllable. We do not discover when she died nor how old the little one was when she lost her natural protectress. Only indirectly can one make conjectures in regard to this peculiarly important point.

Maria was from an early age a marvelous child. "She spoke a language of her own, which only the initiated or a very poetic person could understand. All lifeless things lived for her; she transferred to flowers, trees, buildings, yes, even furniture and clothing the feelings of a human soul. She mixed sense impressions in her speech in the strangest fashion, so that she asserted of tones that they looked red or blue, and inversely of the colors that they sounded cheerful or sad. A girl a few years older than she named her the blue song." Both phenomena, the attributing of life to inanimate things, to which one speaks as to beloved human beings, as well as the phenomenon of synesthesia, color audition and seeing of tone colors, are as we know positively today, to be referred back to erotic motives.[20]

[20] According to my psychoanalytic experience children who cling so to inanimate things see in them either sexual symbols or those things were once objects of their secret sexual enjoyment. It may happen, for example, that such a child falls in love with the furniture, the walls of the room, yes, even a closet, stays there by the hour, kisses the walls, tells them its joys and sorrows and hangs them with all sorts of pictures. One very often sees children talking with inanimate things. They are embarrassed and break off at once if surprised by their elders. If there were not something forbidden behind this, there would be no ground for denying what they are doing, the more so since in fairy tales beasts, plants and also inanimate things speak with mankind and with one another without the child taking offense at it. The latter first becomes confused by the same action when he is pilfering from the tree of knowledge and has something sexual to hide. Hug-Hellmuth has convincingly demonstrated the erotic connection of the child's enthusiasm for plants as well as the different synesthesias. (See her study, "er Farbenhen," Imago, Vol., pp.?18f. Abstracted in Psa. Rev., Vol.I, No.?, January, 1915.)

"With Maria's seventh year perhaps, the tendency to play and purposeless dreaming, which is always bound with such lively, mobile phantasy, gave place, to the astonishment of all, to an exactly opposite tendency. From this time she began to take root in life with all the intensity of her nature. Already in her twelfth or thirteenth year she looked after the father's household, to the admiration of all who beheld her. A divine blessing seemed to accompany everything which she undertook; everything increased under her hands. She could in passing enjoy herself well in the idealistic dreams of the poets and of her acquaintances, but her own peculiar element was reality."

What had produced this sudden turn about? I cannot escape the conjecture that here the death of her mother had a decisive influence and with it the necessity to take the place with her father of his wife. Her housewifely activity is noted first to be sure from her twelfth or thirteenth year. Yet I am of the opinion that she had already in her seventh year begun to play this role--in which year the death of her mother would be placed--only because she was too small it had been under the eye of a maid or housekeeper. My analyses of hysterics has taught me that so profound and sudden a transformation of the whole character always takes place upon definite erotic grounds and for a quite definite erotic purpose.

The earliest love of the tiny maiden belongs almost always to her own father, who is in truth her first beloved. One can often hear it from the child's lips, "You know, Papa, when Mama dies then I will marry you." That is in the childish sense meant quite properly and literally. The early, premature death of the mother gives reality to such infantile wishes, at least as far as concerns the care of the house. As soon then as Maria may begin to play this part, she fills it in a striking and inimitable fashion, although in years she is yet a mere child. She is altogether the mother in the care of a boy outside the family and this, as he quite rightly remarked, laughing boisterously and heartily, even where it is not necessary. Thus her first thought, when she spends her first night banished from home, is of "the poor father, who must go to bed without the little services to which he is so accustomed."

She possesses a maturity in the management of the household which few elders have. Everything goes on and is done without any one noticing that it is being done. "Is there anything more charming than this sixteen year old little house mother in her housekeeping activities?" says one of her admirers. "Just look, let her do what she will, she accomplishes it in the best way and at the same time most beautifully." She is quite contented in the position which she has made. Her eroticism seems completely satisfied. "She is psychically yet so little a woman that there is not the least sexual inclination in the charm that infuses her and therefore her bodily development is overlooked. There is also no trace yet of that entrancing shyness which springs from the mere suspicion that there must be something else about the man." A friend of the family expresses it thus: "When one considers the repose, the self possession of her nature, the freedom from constraint and the spirituality of it, one might almost believe that she was not originally of this earth but perhaps a native of the moon, which seems to exercise more influence upon her than the earth." Every trace of dreamy maiden phantasies, which represent nothing but unconscious love desires, was wanting in her. What she formerly possessed of these was now completely bound with her care of the father.

Her erotic nature is for the time satisfied and needs nothing more to veil it and has nothing to wish for. Therefore she has on the one hand kept childhood's clearness of vision, before which there can be no deceit, on the other hand unbroken contentment with herself and all the world as well as the capacity to forgive immediately every wrong suffered. According to the picture drawn by the poet of the passionate nature of the father, which is capable of hurrying him, the pastor, into reviling God, it seems to me plain why Maria, if she suffered wrong, "is distressed merely over the remorse which the other one, she knows, must feel, when he has finally come to an insight and to reflection." This is nothing else than the father's voice, who had once done wrong to his child and had in a later searching of heart repented of it. Maria, with such early satisfaction of her feelings of love begged "even as a child for nothing which the parents had to refuse her. If she had any need it was to be busy, to take care of the order and the nourishment of the house, the satisfaction and welfare of the inmates. Where she could love, she was happy and at home. Yet even the love for her father never proclaimed itself passionately but always rather in unwearied attention and concern for his smallest need, which only she might suspect as well as for that which manifested itself actively." For herself she scarcely had any wants. A piece of bread and two apples satisfied her as her day's nourishment, which is typical for the hysteric anorexia and perhaps merely signifies the unconscious wish to cost the father as little as possible. Just one single characteristic was wanting for her perfection, the soft, clinging, typically feminine characteristic. This also becomes understandable when one considers that all eroticism toward the father is inhibited in its sexual goal, and may manifest itself only intellectually on account of the incest barrier, at least as far as it comes into consciousness.

The womanly within her shall nevertheless find release through the young Eisener. I have mentioned above how he hung upon his mother. As the early inclination of the small maiden is generally toward the father, so the first love of the boy is for the mother. It is she who teaches him to love and to seek the woman of his heart according to her own image. Later, just before puberty we might say, the boy becomes acquainted with the secrets of sexual life, then, clinging to certain impulses of his childhood, he begins to desire the mother also in the newly acquired sense, while he begins to hate the father as a favored rival, who stands in the way of this wish, and develops a conscious antagonism toward him. He falls, as we say, under the domination of the Oedipus complex. Yet the wishes toward the mother go as a rule no further, since meanwhile the incest barrier has already for a long time been erected. Through this the boy is compelled to submit the mother complex to a splitting. For a moment the phantasy may come to him that the mother shall conduct him into the sexual life--a feature not wanting in any youth--but it is now decidedly rejected or more typically displaced upon those women who make of love a profession and actually take care to initiate the youth into the sexual life. For this reason the remainder of the mother complex is idealized and the mother transformed to a pure virgin woman, toward whom no man dares direct his desire. Similarly is it with the loved one, whom one chooses after the pattern of the mother.

So Eisener expresses himself warmly. "Maria is not made for love, only for reverence."

Yet without the child's craving for the mother[21] he would not have become a compulsive neurotic,[22] with all the hypermorality of the latter, pride in his moral purity and extravagant self reproaches, even a lustful self laceration after he had at one single time been overpowered by sensuality. Furthermore his lack of resoluteness, decisiveness and courage is not, as he mentions, the result of his myopia but of his neurosis. He has developed himself, out of an unconscious rivalry, in direct contrast to his intensely narrow-minded father. The latter was only a tradesman, who set his comfort above everything, for whom art had value only in so far as it increased his own enjoyment of life. So painting becomes the son's chief delight in spite of his exaggerated myopia or perhaps just on account of it. He bore his father's tyranny with difficulty[23] and with inner protest. His tendency toward the free kingdom of art stood in contrast to him, and in the same way he sought on the other hand a substitute for the mother in every woman. He offered up for his sin the dreams of his youth when he first believed that his moral nature was stained and became as a result, as even the elder feels uneasily, an over obedient son.

[21] One thinks of Eisener's panegyric: "Before her clear look confusion cannot exist, the coarse word of insolence sinks back unspoken into the shame filled breast. The brightness of a lost paradise shines from her eyes upon the fallen bringing pain and warning, the consolation of eternal pity smiles upon the penitent."

[22] Like Otto Ludwig himself.

[23] The well-known psychic overcompensation in congenital organic inferiority.

How had this so easily befallen him with a mother so deeply honored! Around her spun all the boy's love desire and twined itself about her, and all that lava heated feeling belonging so peculiarly to the child alone. He had hung upon that idol the longing of his heart, the phantasies of a power of imagination lustfully excited, which is not indeed wanting in the best of children, although commonly these are inhibited, and later even completely forgotten because of restraining moral impulses. Therefore the memory of the highly honored mother is awakened not only through Maria, the pure one, but also through Julie, who comes into contact with his sensual desire and the unclean childish phantasies slumbering in the last analysis behind this. It is interesting how strikingly the poet is able to point out that double emotion in Eisener's soul.

There the moral restraining impulses were first crowded back by the wine plentifully pressed upon him, which he, accustomed from his early years to moderation, could tolerate in only the smallest amount. Now "the sly Julie seemed to him ever more charming. A play of glances began between the two, which appeared to make the young hunter jealous. On the other hand Eisener himself felt something similar when his neighbor on the left addressed to the earnest Maria words which did not conceal the liking she had inspired. He listened to her replies almost with fear and was delighted that there was not audible in them the least response to this inclination, and then he wondered at himself over this same division in his nature. In Julie's dark eyes glowed a flame, of which he felt how it kindled him and that its fire must attract more and more to itself without his being able to defend himself from it, yes, without his wishing to be able to do it." To be sure when "the slender Maria stood like a holy picture behind Julie, the alluring child of the world with all her seductive graces sank low in value in contrast to the former. He felt the need to be open with himself." Transparency was a necessity to him from his youth, as an inheritance from his wise mother. "Then Breitung thrust with his glass against Eisener's refilled one. Laughing and drinking he found the motley interchange of the liveliest ideas outwardly, which already had taken the place of quiet thought, soon becoming less and less menacing and finally even agreeable and desirable."

His sexual excitement, heightened besides through the plentiful indulgence in alcohol and the general boisterousness, was brought to a high pitch by an episode with the passionate Julie. Eisener had to leave the room with her during a social game. "A strange thing happened to him, for as he bent down in the adjoining room in the dark to the quick breathing Julie, instead of her ear her burning mouth met his mouth, and the soft pulsating form fell as if fainting into his arms. Wrestling with himself, striving to keep his senses, he seized her arm involuntarily and stood again with her in the assembly room before he was conscious what it was all about."

Is not this behavior of the youth burning with desire peculiarly strange? What if behind it there is fixed a memory perhaps of a scene with the mother, who brought him to his senses by seizing his arm? Yet, it might always be so for him, he had found the power once more to withstand the hot temptation. Not to be sure without subsequent regret. For when he later sought his room he could not go to sleep and "his phantasy conjured up again, as often as he resisted it, that dark room about him and the bewitching Julie in his arms. He regretted a thousand times, so much did he distress himself, his joy at his instinctive flight, that he had not drunk that sweet poison to the full, whose mere touch had brought his whole being to this feverish pulsation."

He sought now to find cooling for his heated blood in the garden, and in fact the fragrance of the flowers and the rustling of the leaves so soothed his excited mind that gradually the sense of a pleasant languor came over him. In a half unconsciousness he went upstairs again and back to bed. He was just falling asleep when he saw a white form enter, whose features he could not make out because of his shortsightedness. As it disrobed and came toward him, he first, as if seeking for help, reached with his hands toward the side where his friend should be sleeping. He did not however find him, he apparently had been put into another room. "The thought of being alone for the first time with a womanly being in the security of night crept over him at first like icecold drops, then like the glow of fire over all his nerves. His heart pounded audibly as the figure climbed into his bed. The strangeness and adventure of the situation was not fitted to work rationally upon the intoxicated man, whose excitement throbbed into his finger tips. The power of the warning inner voice disappeared with his reason and the strife was brief before nature came off conqueror."

I have before this sketched Maria's character development up to the time when Eisener came into her life. Yet one point may be added. She had retained one single influence from her childhood in spite of all change in her seventh year, which "with the beginning of maturity appeared only occasionally and as it were in secret. The moon had been her dearly beloved and her desire; as a small child she had been able to look at the moon for hours without intermission. If she was sick her mother or nurse must carry her to the window through which she might look upon the friend of her small soul." About half a year before her acquaintance with Eisener "the moon had made its influence felt upon her sleep, as it had before affected her waking. At the time of the full moon she often left her couch, dressed herself and went up into the corner room in the pavilion. Here she stood for some time and turned her closed eyes toward the moon. Then she dropped the curtain, undressed and lay down in the bed, which stood in the spot where she had been used to sleep as a child. As soon as the moon had left the windows of this room or shone through the windows of her present sleeping room, she arose again, dressed herself and returned. She herself knew nothing of these wanderings, and whatever was done to awaken her during them was in vain. The physician thought that these attacks of moon walking would disappear finally when maturity was established, or at least at her first confinement."

In this picture from a layman are some new and striking features. First is the love--one can call it nothing else--which the child bestows upon the planet. Why is the moon her beloved and her desire from childhood up, why can she stand by the hour looking at it, why does she long when sick to be laid so that she can look at it all the time? He who observes children knows that such extreme love, which endures for years without wearying of it, and finally that ability to stare steadily at the moon, must have a sexual content, although naturally no one will admit this. Only when the object, in our case the heavenly body, is sexually stimulating is the love for it enduring for all time, undergoing no change, no abatement of feeling for it. As Maria's erotism later found satisfaction in her father, her love toward the moon steadily receded. But at the entrance upon puberty her sexual impulse increased and she began to wander in the moonlight. The love finally which Eisener inspires in her, together with the strong sexual excitement, which the f 阝今 e the day before had called forth in her, occasions again an attack, in which she surrenders herself willingly to the beloved.

The folk, like the family physician, have not a doubt of the sexual basis of the moon mania with her as with individuals in general. When puberty is established or she has a child of her own the attacks will cease, is the opinion of the latter. The servant maid Grete also, a living book of fairy tales among her people, explains the moon wandering as nothing else than the result of an unsatisfied sense desire. There was a young knight who had wooed a rich woman of gentle birth. Shortly before midnight they were both led into the bridal chamber. "Yet hardly were they alone together when a strange voice outside before the castle called, 'Conrad, come down here! Conrad, come down here!' And again it called, 'Conrad, come down here!' The voice sounded so plaintive and at the same time so threatening. The bridegroom said, 'That is my best friend; he is in need and calls me.' The maiden said however, 'The voice belongs to my cousin, who was found dead two years ago.' Then she shuddered so that the gooseflesh stood up over her whole body," and she implored her bridegroom not to follow the evil spirit or at least to remain with her until the ghostly hour was past and the full moon was up. But he would not be restrained: "Be it an evil spirit or a good, no one shall call me in vain!" "And he went out. The lady went to the window but could see nothing for the darkness outside and for the tears in her eyes. Then the haunted hour was over and the full moon arose and she waited and waited, but the knight never returned. Thereupon she swore to take no rest on a night when the moon was full until she had gone to bed with her bridegroom. And as her first bridegroom never and nevermore came back, so she waited for another, but there was no one who knew her story who would woo her, because each one thought it would fare with him as it had fared with that other. Thus she died; her oath is however still unfulfilled. Whenever it is full moon, she is looking out to see if any bridegroom comes and she laments sorely, and holds her hands weeping toward the moon."

In this folk tale the exclusively sexual foundation of the wandering is quite plainly expressed. The ghost makes use of a voice, complaining and threatening at the same time, which the bridegroom believes to be the call for help of his best friend, and the bride on the other hand imagines it the voice of her cousin, who had been found dead two years before, perhaps after she had taken her own life because unhappy in love. Both may be driven by sexual jealousy--I offer this as a hypothesis--which would not permit the other sexual gratification which is denied to himself or herself, the friend perhaps meaning jealousy from a homosexual tendency. The ghost having accomplished its purpose at the hour of midnight and in the light of the full moon, the lady swore "to take no rest on a night when the moon was full until she had gone to bed with her bridegroom." That is the kernel of the entire myth, the na 囮 e and yet apparently conclusive folk interpretation of the riddle of moon walking, at least in its most frequent form.

I have above taken it for granted that Maria's erotism was satisfied through her care for her father. That must of course be understood with some qualification. For she could play the role of mother only as housekeeper, not as wife. The former is satisfying therefore only so long, until stronger sexual impulses awaken through external stimuli or, according to rule, through the natural development of a maiden. When once that has come to pass, one so disposed to it as Maria was, begins to wander in the moonlight. Why then, it may further be asked, does Maria seek for her childhood bed, if the goal and the aim of the wandering is the sexual satisfaction of the maiden? In the case analyzed at the beginning the compelling motive was a sexual self stimulation upon the mother, in later years in the loved object whoever it was, male or female. In most cases, since normal sexual feeling predominates, the aim of the sleep walking is that of the folk tale, to go to bed with the lover. That would explain without difficulty the scene of the union in Maria's case, as soon as she had come to know Eisener.

But what lay specially at the foundation of her earlier wandering, when no man had yet made an impression upon her? Or was there perhaps one, in relation to whom sexuality is most strongly forbidden, her own father? What if her erotic desire toward him was repressed and the indifference which she had attained was transferred over to all men? Much that is apparently harmless is permitted to a child, which would be regarded with horror in the adult. Many parents like to take their children into bed early in the morning and play with them without any consciously sexual thoughts and without suspecting how very often they in this way stimulate sexual desire in their children. Frequently also the mother or father visit the child before going to sleep, lean over the bed, allow themselves often to press the child passionately to themselves and count this asexual love toward the child. The case analyzed at the beginning teaches us how much of the grossly sexual erotic is concealed behind this, even if well hidden. Maria likewise sought presumably in her sleep walking for the bed of her childhood because her earliest erotism was bound with it.

This had already happened under the instigation of puberty, before her heart had spoken. How is it now since she loves Eisener? We must keep in mind her unconscious wish, to climb into the bed of the man she loves, and on the other hand that Maria as housemother knew well that he was not sleeping alone, but with his friend, so only a compromise form of action would be possible. So she goes up again to her childhood room, which lies in the same direction as Eisener's sleeping room. There she first draws the curtain aside that she may gaze at the moon, which increases the sexual excitement with her, as I have earlier discussed. Then she undresses before the mirror as she probably had done as a child, and moves forward toward the beloved one, who after a brief struggle with himself embraces her passionately. She nevertheless submits to his caresses without response but also without resistance. For thus alone can the fiction be maintained that she has loved without consciousness of it and therefore also without culpability. It is not difficult, according to the analysis of the first case, to understand how she finally at the withdrawal of the moonlight gets up again, dresses herself before the mirror and leaves the room as noiselessly as she had entered it.

The later portions of the narrative must confirm my assumptions if they are correct, that Eisener merely embraces the mother in Maria and that she on the other hand knows well enough in the unconscious both as child and as maiden that she wishes for that which is sexually forbidden and knows whom she desires. Let us see what the poet tells us. As Eisener awakes after the bridal night, he is not at all invigorated and uplifted as otherwise a man in like case, but psychically and physically cast down, as if he had to atone for some great wrong. "He strove to consider the strange adventure of this night as the delusion of a fevered dream. Yet that adventure painted itself before him, in spite of all his effort to forget it, in ever more vivid colors," because indeed a wish of his heart had been fulfilled through it. His inner unrest drove him forth and, as walking about he met his beloved, he marveled "that Maria seemed taller to him today than yesterday, or rather that he believed that he first noticed today that she was tall." What could this mean except that Maria now seemed big to him as once the mother had seemed to the small boy? Only he had first to embrace his beloved, before he could perceive such a thing and give heed to it. Maria herself, who apparently had enjoyed her pleasure only in her sleep and unconsciously, and therefore knew nothing of it all, had lost her frank manner with him, which she still possessed the day before. She grew red at his look and drew the hand which she gave him "quickly back again in confused fear," without consciously knowing why. "The flower of womanhood which had slumbered in her too serene, too cold image, appeared in this one night to have come with magic swiftness to bud and immediately to have unfolded in all its fragrance." Maria herself pictures her condition: "That morning I can never forget. Everything was so still, so solemn; the guests were all yet asleep. I had never been so strong of heart. I felt that morning as if all my life before had been only a dream and life was now just beginning. It seemed to me that I had suddenly become grown up and was now for the first time a child no more." Maria thus felt herself through the bridal night to have grown up from the child to the mother, only, now, it was for the lover who had taken the father's place.

Both Eisener and Maria conducted themselves further entirely in accordance with their earlier unconscious wishes. The former for example "found a growing pleasure in representing his own action, when it was really the effect of many circumstances acting one upon the other, as the result of a cold, calm calculation on his part." And was it not at bottom actually something like a calculation, since he in his earliest childhood phantasies imagined something similar for himself from the mother? It is only natural that he now greatly exaggerated in consciousness the sin which he had desired. Never for a moment did it occur to him "to throw any part of the burden of guilt upon that being who so closely participated in it. His rightful feeling remained in regard to it that he had this night given to a woman a right to himself, which he, if she should demand it, could not dispute. It was a source of calmness to him to look upon himself as punished, as it were, in this manner." Only all too evident! This punishment was in reality a disguised reward, fulfilment of the infantile wish to win the mother.[24] For this reason he had not been able earlier to withstand Julie although Maria attracted him far more. For the former was the indulgent mother of his power of imagination, the latter on the contrary the proud, unapproachable mother of his real childhood. Moreover, though he did not conceal from himself that his heart belonged to the chaste Maria, yet he resolved, if Julie should convince him that she had been the ghostly visitor, to offer her his hand immediately. "The doubt, whether she deserved it, which was near enough at hand, he put from him as an excuse which he wished to make so that he could believe that he might release himself from that which he had to recognize as his duty."

Maria however "he had in these days accustomed himself to think of as a being so high above him that his love must profane her." Again the well known splitting of the mother into the holy and the yielding one.

[24] Cf. with this also the interesting passage ... "the passionate self accusations, in torturing himself with which he found comfort a short time before."

How did it appear at this time to her, herself? The first weeks after that moonlight night the woman in her bloomed forth more and more, in spite of the fact that her lover tarried at a distance. Yet when in her body a new life began to develop and Eisener still did not appear, she was seized suddenly with a hysterical convulsion--she was wearing significantly the same rose-colored dress in which he had seen her that morning--which lasted twelve hours so that every one looked upon her as dead. The despairing father threw himself across her feet and lay there--a situation which will occupy us later--and Eisener, who was just now returning, was driven by the bitterest self reproaches across the ocean. After waking from her catalepsy Maria did not regain her former blooming health but grew more and more ill, which the family physician finally discovered as the result of her pregnancy.

"The good girl herself believed at first that what she felt and what they told her was a vivid troubled dream." This idea will not appear strange to us who know so much about moon walking and that one does everything merely "in sleep" in order to remain blameless. "That she should become a mother seemed to her so strange and wonderful that she appeared to herself as some one else (this might well read, as her own mother dead at so early an age) or as suddenly transplanted into another world with strange people, animals and trees. The sound of her own voice, the tone of the bells seemed to her as other and strange sounds." We may bring forward in explanation in this place the case analyzed at the beginning, where a moon walker had abandoned herself to all sorts of dreams. In the moon must be living men of another sort with other feelings, customs and manners, and the sexual, strongly forbidden upon earth, must be freely permitted upon this planet. She seemed to herself on account of her sexual phantasies already as a child quite different from other people, as if she belonged not upon this earth but upon the moon. Could not a similar thought process have taken place with Maria?

I said of her father, that he had been her first beloved. And it comes almost as an unconscious recognition of this when he, filled with anger, calls out to her mockingly, "Why do you not say that the whole affair has come to pass out of love to me, to prepare for me an unexpected joy?" Breitung also enjoyed since her earliest childhood her unlimited confidence only on this account because he loved her as his own child. Therefore she looks up with all her anxiety so trustfully and self confidently to this friend of her father. But when Breitung also no longer believed in her and her father turned from her with scorn it was "as if all her blood streamed into her eyes that, pressing out as tears, it might relieve her. Yet here it remained and pressed upon her brain as if threatening its fibers. With a strangely fearful haste she pressed her eyes with her fingers; they remained dry; a cry of pain would unburden her soul-- no sound accompanied the trembling, convulsive breathing. The old servant, who entered after a while, found her lying with her breast upon the sofa pillow, her head thrown violently back," in hysterical opisthotonos. "The old man had loved Maria from her earliest childhood" and stood accordingly in the place of a father. "He clasped his hands together in distress. She recognized him and suffered him patiently to bring her head to a less forced position. She looked at him sharply as if she would convince herself that he was the one she took him to be. His Kalmuck features seemed to her as beautiful as the soul which they hid and seemed to want to disown.

"The friendliness, the affectionate regard, which spoke so unmistakably out of the familiar old graybearded, sunburnt face, did her no end of good." Since she could not yet entirely believe she asked, "Is it indeed you, Justin? And you will still recognize me? And you do not flee from me?" At first the deplorable commission which the old man had to carry out threw her back again. When she had to understand that her father would not again set foot in the pastor's house until she had departed, her countenance became deathly pale and convulsive movements trembled in quick succession over her delicate body so that the old man wept aloud, for he believed that she had gone mad. His signs of distress, the faithfulness and love which spoke through them, touched her so effectually that at last the hysterical convulsion relaxed and she sank down. "The old man caught her up. He placed her on the sofa. She lay across his lap; her head lay upon his left hand, with the other he held her body fast that it should not slip to the floor. It seemed as if she would weep her whole weary self away. The old servant held her with trembling hand and heavy heart." Now the scene of childhood is complete, except that the old man plays the role of her father. So had Maria presumably done as a child when she felt too unhappy and so also the pastor's throwing himself down, as we saw above, over his daughter whom he believed dead, is not strange.

When Maria had left the parsonage her first thought and silent concern was how her father must now live without her care, even that perhaps he would not be there any more, when everything had later turned out well. Then she thought again of the time when she would be a mother and "her life seemed to her as a tale that is told." On her journey to her new home there came over her ever more strongly "the feeling of her complete abandonment. All the dear childhood memories, into whose protection she would flee, turned in anger from her. With tears she cried to God for a heart that she might love, some one for whom she might really care. For it seemed as if a curse lay upon her, which estranged all hearts from her. She thought with fear at her heart that the being to whom she would give life might likewise turn from her, as everything had done that she loved." Then a good fate brings to her the unfortunate Johannes whom his crazy father wished to throw into the water in order to preserve him for eternal happiness. At once Maria assumes the role of mother toward the boy and now "that once more she had to care for some one, she was again the calm and serene being."

What had so thrown her out of her course? It was not so much the banishment from the father's house, not the contempt of all the world, nor even of her very oldest and truest friend. She would have been able to look beyond both of these, because her consciousness felt itself entirely blameless. But she took so to herself the truth that she was no more the loving, caretaking house mother nor might play that part, that for a brief while she planned to take her life. She prayed to God with tears for one heart only that she might love, that she might actually care for. Since the care of her father is taken from her she feels herself at first truly and utterly forlorn, all the dear memories of childhood turn in anger from her and a curse seems to rest upon her soul.

Why do all the memories of her childhood turn from her, if she actually knows herself guiltless? Is this merely because the father is indissolubly bound with them? If she still consciously feels entirely blameless toward him, and if he openly did her wrong from a false assumption, then should not the childhood memories return to her? I think the solution must be sought elsewhere, in this, that Maria knew nothing in clear consciousness of the happenings of that moonlight night and could honestly swear to that, but everything was known in the unconscious. Here is the sense of guilt engendered, of which consciousness may know nothing, here she knows well enough that the youthful Eisener has embraced her and she has together with him deceived the father whom she first loved. The goal of all moon walking is none other than to be able to enjoy and still be blameless, it is blamelessness because without accompanying consciousness.

The poet's words must confirm this, if this assumption is correct. We will test them. The first night of her banishment Maria, while going to sleep, thought first of her father "who must go to bed without the little services which he was accustomed to receive from her." Then she thought of Breitung and the apothecary's daughter, who had turned from her full of scorn. "The young Eisener occurred to her in the midst of this, she knew not how, and a sort of curiosity whether Eisener also would have turned from her in so unfriendly a fashion as Breitung. She pictured to herself how he might have looked upon her now with contempt, now with friendliness, as on that morning which she so gladly remembered." Also an evident identification of the young Eisener with the father and the father's friend, and flight from the loved ones who had cast her off to him who had inclined to her as a friend.

Yet more convincing is a passage which follows. Maria had born a son and "the more she looked with joy upon the small infant contemplating his sound and beautiful body, the more grew the need within her, only instinctively felt at first, to have some one who could rejoice in the child with her, not out of mere sympathy with her, but because he had the same right to it and so that she could rejoice again in his joy, as he might in hers. Without knowing how and why, she thought again of the friendly and true hearted Eisener. Her dreams brought his picture before her eyes in most vivid colors. It seemed as if it were Eisener who should enjoy the child with her. She hastened to him with tears of joy to lay the beautiful boy in his arms, and when she now stood by him, she had scarcely the heart to show him the boy. Then she cast down her eyes and said confusedly, 'See this beautiful child, Eisener, Sir!'" Maria knew quite well in the unconscious that she had conceived her child from Eisener and the sudden restraint when she laid the boy in his arms is only a compromise with consciousness, which must not know the facts, otherwise she could not be spared her feeling of guilt. Yes, when Julie then came with her love child, which she had conceived that same moonlight night from the hunter, although she really loved Eisener, then "Maria experienced, she knew not why, a gentle aversion toward her. She said quietly, 'That in which one has done no wrong and cannot change, one must bear patiently.'"

Soon however there awoke a desire in her "for something new, still unknown to her, which she nevertheless felt must come now. It was the strange, fearfully sweet condition of the ripeness of love, which had not yet found the object on which she could open her heart. That night a need awakened, formerly repressed into the background by greater pain, but which threatened now to outgrow other desires and feelings in the undisputed possession of him." Often she sat knitting and dreaming at the boy's cradle. "There was a fair at Marklinde. She went early in her rose-colored dress into the garden and plucked wild hedge roses. She was startled for she heard a noise behind her and she knew that it was Eisener who was coming after her. She turned into another path; she was afraid to meet him, and yet she wished that he would follow her. As she bent low behind some flowers, she threw a hasty look behind her. She grew rosy because he might have noticed the look, and still it would have made her glad if he had noticed it. 'Yet if he knew everything,' she whispered to herself; 'but I could not tell him, nor could I let him perceive it. I would have to say No, although he understood it as Yes!' Suddenly he stood near her; he had seized her hand and was looking into her eyes. She bowed her head, he bent toward her. It seemed so strange to her--their lips touched--Maria frightened and blushing, sprang involuntarily from her chair, as if what she was dreaming were real.

"A strangely mingled feeling drove her from her chair to the window and from the window back to the chair. She felt herself stirred in her very depths by something which wounded her sensibility as much as it excited her longing. She fled to her child. She strove to think of something else; in vain. That thought continually returned and gradually lost its frightful character. Soon she felt it only as a sweet dread and so the idea received a double stimulation while it woke the curious question, why and for what reason she must really be afraid. And as she looked now upon the child, it seemed to her so marvellous that she, mother and yet maiden, knew nothing of the happiness of which this little life must be the fruit. Julie's words were continually ringing in her ears, 'The happiness which is granted him, has to be reckoned too dear.' It gave her unending satisfaction, to think of herself actually in such a situation to the young Eisener that all her unhappiness was the result of a joy which she had granted him, without knowing what joy this must have been." I consider it superfluous to add a word to complete the interpretation of these phantasies, which speak for themselves. They confirm everything that I have said above, better than any labored explanation. Later Maria came to know that what had sustained her in the hours of her sorrow was nothing else than that mysterious but certain premonition of a happy life with Eisener and her George.

And now back to the purpose of the analysis of all these tales. What does it teach us for the understanding of moon walking? First of all it confirms many of our earlier conclusions. The most important thing, in the first place, is that sexual impulses lie at the foundation, desire for sexual gratification, and that one apparently acts in sleep in order to escape all culpability, while the unconscious still knows all about it. The sleep walking begins, in accordance with the sexual basic motive, at the time of puberty and lasts until it is inhibited by the close of that period or in women with the birth of the first child. It is further established that at the beginning the bed of childhood is sought, the place of earlier sexual pleasures, later however the bed of the loved object, who appears in the place of the originally loved object, the parent. Finally, moreover, when the night wanderer fixes his closed eyes upon the moon before starting out on his wandering, erotic thoughts hide behind this, which in turn go back to earliest childhood. The heavenly body effects a sexual excitement not only through its light, but indeed also through sexual phantasies which are bound with it. Lastly folk myth knows likewise that the woman in white represents nothing else than the maiden in her night shift with all her sexual longings.

One thing more this novel also confirms, which our earlier discoveries have already taught us, the abnormal muscle excitability and muscle erotic. For Maria was seized with a hysterical convulsion when her father's unkindness pressed itself upon her. It is interesting that this abnormal muscle excitability, which manifested itself in various muscular convulsions, was present with Otto Ludwig throughout his earthly career. Already as a boy he often suffered convulsive muscular twitchings, when he had exceptional tasks to perform or hard thinking was required of him, and "nervous twitchings of the head" are recorded of him when twenty-three years old, also presumably a tic had won for him the nickname of "the shaker." Later moreover our poet suffered chronically from convulsive manifestations of a lesser degree, repeatedly however in a stronger, special form although only in temporary attacks.[25]

[25] Cf. with this especially Ernst Jentsch, "Das Pathologische bei Otto Ludwig," "Grenzfragen des Nerven- und Seelenlebens," published by L. Lenfeld, No.?0.

In other words, it may be said that Ludwig assigns to Maria and the young Eisener a series of his own personal characteristics. That is to say, not only was the tendency to convulsive attacks peculiar to him, but also to fainting, and a compulsive neurotic and hysterical tendency, the high grade myopia, a fondness for discussing painting, talking with inanimate things,[26] colored audition, as well as other synesthesias, and finally a special reverence for his mother.

[26] Cf. here the poet's words: "It is strange that nature is personified for me, that I not only live in her, but as one human being with another, exchanging, not merely receiving, thoughts and feelings, and even so, that different places become as individual to me, distinct from others and, as it were, transformed in consciousness, so that I not only feel that they effect an influence upon me but it seems to me as if I work upon them, and the forms, as they appear to me, show the traces of this influence." Further: "I ... who stood even in a wonderful mutual understanding with mountain and flora, because the kingdom of love was not to be restrained...."

"BUSCHNOVELLE," by Otto Ludwig.

The moon plays an important part in the romance just discussed, even apart from Maria's night wandering, and a number of significant events take place under its very light. We find this relationship still stronger in Otto Ludwig's "Buschnovelle," briefly referred to earlier, which I add here, though it really does not directly treat of our problems. The heroine Pauline passed with many as moon struck and her blue eyes "have a strange expression of their own. They gaze as aliens upon this world, as angels, which, transplanted to our marvelous earth, belong to the heavenly home and cannot find themselves amid this confused and agitated humanity." Likewise his bride asserts of the count that he knows no other recreation "than to climb about in the night over the rocks and worship the moon." This perhaps gave occasion to the rumor of a ghost or at least breathed new life into an old tale.

A prince was banished under an enchantment to the rocks of the gods. He had "a face as of a person twenty years old or so, but pale and quite transparent like moonlight, and he could be rescued only through a maiden eighteen years old and as innocent as when she came from the mother's womb." The count, whom his bride deceived, became very melancholy over it and trusted no woman after this. He learned to know and love Pauline upon the rocks of the gods, where he was accustomed to wander in the moonlight. When she believed she saw in him the enchanted prince and declared her intention of voluntarily rescuing him, he stipulated that she must climb down from off the rocks, down from the cross, without touching them with her hands but holding her arms toward the full moon. "And that must take place tomorrow night when the moon is sailing overhead, otherwise I must remain enchanted. When you shall have climbed down the rocks, I shall be saved and then I will make you my princess." One may read afterward from the poet how Pauline then carried out her resolve--her determination alone, sprung evidently from a great love, had already cured the count of his sadness--how the count saved her and later wooed her.

Emphasis will be laid here merely upon two facts, first that not only all important events happen in the light of the full moon, but that also no other novel shows so many autobiographical features. The most recent publisher of this tale, Heinrich Borcherdt, gives this explanation: "One can recognize without much trouble in the portrait of the count with his well-trimmed beard the poet himself, who at that time tended to great seriousness and to melancholy. For this very reason the cheerfulness, gaiety and unrestrained naturalness of his bride Emilie worked most refreshingly upon him. Pauline in the tale exercised a similar influence upon the count. What we know of Emilie Ludwig from without agrees likewise with the picture of Pauline. Pauline's father suggests Emilie's father.... The greatest weight will be laid upon the fact that we possess in this work a poetic glorification of Otto Ludwig's love happiness in Triebischtal. The rural life is reproduced in every detail." Nothing unfortunately is reported in the different sketches of his life whether and how far the poet and his bride allowed themselves to be influenced by the light of the full moon. The striking fact remains at any rate that twice in the course of two years he spun out this theme and each time moreover with a strongly autobiographical note. That cannot be sufficiently explained merely through the influence of Tieck, whom he, to be sure, read diligently in his youth.

"LEBENSMAGIE, WIRKLICHKEIT UND TRAUM," by Theodor Mundt ("Life's Magic, Reality and Dream").

In the seventh volume of the "Euphorion" Richard M. Meyer has exhumed a probable source of Ludwig's "Maria." It is a fictitious tale of the "young German" Theodor Mundt, which appeared in his collection "Charaktere und Situationen" in 1837, five years before the "Maria," and shows in fact some external similarities with this. Still Otto Ludwig expressly acknowledges a tale told by a friend as the source, but gives no syllable of mention to Mundt. I must say that it seems at least very questionable that the latter's story was the model, although the Berlin literary historian comes to the conclusion, "A direct utilization would be here difficult to dispute." I will reproduce the contents of this story, as far as it touches our problems, as closely as possible in the words of Mundt, although this story, which is contained in the collection mentioned under the separate title of "Lebensmagie, Wirklichkeit und Traum," hardly possesses an artistic value.

The theological student Emil Hahn had, as one of his friends states, "lost life itself over his books and before his merry companions, who would have initiated him into the true enjoyment of existence, crowed many a moral cock-a-doodle-doo of virtue and self restraint." On the ride home to his father and foster sister Rosalinde he was urged by two student acquaintances to a little drinking bout, at which he partook of more wine than was good for him. The two comrades sang the praises of Rosalinde, whom Hahn had left as a fourteen year old girl and who in the two years of separation had blossomed out in full beauty. As Hahn returned to the father's house in a half intoxicated state and met Rosalinde in an adjacent room, he found at once, in contrast to his shyness of former times, the courage to approach her. "Ardently and daringly he embraced her and the passionate kiss which he impressed upon her maidenly lips was followed, as one lightning flash succeeds another, by a second more lingering one, which was reluctant to leave off." After he had for some time, again quite contrary to his custom, held his own place at the large party which his father was giving that very evening, "he felt himself gradually seized with weariness and the lively and excited mood, to which the wine he had enjoyed had awakened him, began little by little to disappear with the intoxication. He made his adieus in a dejected tone and betook himself with heavy, hanging head to his room, there to recover himself through sleep, which he could no longer withstand because of his painful state.

"It was late in the night when Emil sprang from his bed. A vivid dream seemed to have confused and frightened him. He stood half clothed in the middle of his room and stared straight ahead as if trying to recollect himself. Above in the night sky glowed the full round moon with a sharp ray seldom seen and its white silver light pierced directly over the head of the youth walking in his sleep. The room gleamed brightly in the moonbeams trembling with mystery, which had spun themselves out in long, glimmering threads over floor and ceiling. Emil had fastened his eyes upon the great disk of the moon and staggered with uncertain steps to the window to open it." While he stood thus there came a small snow white cat--the cat is well known as a favorite animal of the romantic writers--and spoke to him: "I am come to congratulate you on your bridal night. Yes, yes, I know well that you are married. This is a beautiful night to be married. The moon shoots down right warmly, and its strong shining stings the blood and we cats also feel the impulses stirring in the whispering May night. Happy one, you who are married! Married to Rosalinde!"

"Emil, distracted, clasped his forehead. Everything which he saw about him appeared to him changed and even the inanimate things in his vicinity seemed in this moment to have been drawn into a magic alliance. Everything, the very table, chair, press looked at him, rocking themselves saucily in the bright moonlight, personally and familiarly, and had to his eyes, arms and feet to move about, mouths to speak with, senses for communication. At the same time a fair picture rose before the youth deep out of the bottom of his heart, at which he smiled longingly. It was the recollection of Rosalinde and her matured beauty. She passed like a burning, ominous dream through his soul and he felt himself drunken, trembling, exultingly united with the proud but now subdued maiden in a love thrilled bridal night. While he was thus lost in thought his look was held chained by a painting, which hung on the wall opposite him. Strange, it was Rosa's portrait and he knew not whether this picture had just now arisen warm with life merely out of the force of the idea which was kindling him, or whether it had actually been formed over there in its golden frame by a painter's hand." Then the cat mewed again: "That is your young wife Rosalinde. The moonbeam chases her; see how its brightness kisses her temples unceasingly. The young woman is queen on her bridal night. We will crown her, all we who are here in this room and owe our life to the brightness of the moonlight night, we will crown her. I present her for her bridal crown burning, tender desires." Then the May blossoms in the room bestirred themselves and conferred upon her the bloom of fond innocence for her bridal crown. Also the bird in the cage made himself understood: "I give her for her bridal crown the score of my latest melody. Harmony and melody should be the dower of all young brides." Finally a cockchafer also which flew in offered her for her bridal crown "a pair of lovely crickets."

"The dreaming Emil, surrounded by these fairy treasures of the May night, stood in sweet intoxication opposite the glowing picture, bathed in moonlight, of the maiden to whom all this homage belonged. The longer and the more vividly he pictured to himself and leaned toward all the maidenly charms, which had allowed the first passionate wish in the young man's phantasy to blaze up, the more an impatience, almost consuming, pounding, benumbing his heart, seized him, which he did not know how to explain and had never felt before in his life. Like a seductively sweet poison the delusion imparted itself secretly to him that Rosalinde was his bride, his wife, and that this wondrously beautiful spring night, bright with moonlight, was his wedding night. His heart swelled with mighty, growing desire, youthful passion breathed high in him. Trembling, fearful, wavering, longing, he still felt himself strangely happy.

"Then it seemed to him that Rosalinde's picture began to move, as if the gleaming shoulders lifted themselves gradually and gently at first from it. Then the delicate outline of the bosom rose as the lovely form came forth, the face streaming with love bowed itself in modest shame before him. The form grew larger, rose to full beauty, stretched itself to life size. Smiling, beckoning, gazing at him full of mystery, promising favor and happiness, she took some steps toward him, then fled back again ashamed and as if frightened, floated away with sylphlike movements to the door and remained hidden behind it, yet peeping and looking out at the youth.

"He did not know if he should, if he might follow her. He was drawn powerfully after her and yet he stood still and hesitated. The bright moonlight seemed, like a fairy toward one enchanted, to make merry at the loud anxious beating of his heart. He restrained himself no longer; with a passionate movement he hastened with open arms to the beloved apparition, desiring to embrace her, throw himself upon her bosom, breathe out upon her his burning desire. She fled, he followed her. She fled before him, but softly and alluringly and he, intoxicated, rushed after her from room to room unable to overtake the form flitting on with ghostly swiftness. Like a star drawing him onward she floated there before him, his footsteps were as if bewitched by her running, and thus she led him after her, on and on, through a succession of rooms, so that he marveled and thought himself wandering about in a great, unfamiliar enchanted palace.

"At last he saw her no more, the lovely picture had suddenly disappeared from him. He must however still hasten and hasten, there was no rest for him. He no longer knew himself what he was seeking and what he hoped to find. But now he ran upon a door; it opened and he entered a small, cosy room in which stood a white bed. Seized with a strange apprehension the youth drew back the curtains with bold hand, and looked, astonished, smiling, burning with bliss. There lay a beautiful maiden asleep and dreaming--ah! it was Rosalinde herself. In the sweet forgetfulness of sleep, unveiling herself like the outblown petals of a rosebud, she revealed her most secret charms in lovely fulness to the eye of night. Emil stood before her in the dear delusion of aroused passion and bent over her. 'Is not tonight my bridal night?', thought he. He reflected and the hot tumult of exulting senses tore him irresistibly. Then he flung himself passionately into her arms, pressed his mouth to her mouth in yearning kisses and clung closer and closer to the warm, living delight of her charming form. He dared the boldest work of love. The sleeper did not oppose the daring beginning; in the power of a dream, like him, according to the myth, whom the chaste Luna had seized, she seemed at first to yield softly to the seductive moment. Only a glowing color suffused the tender cheek, a gentle halting exclamation breathed through the half open lips. The bright light of the full moon shone on high with its trembling beams directly over the couch of the maiden.

"Now, now however she awakes from the strange troubled dream. She opens her eyes, she shakes her beautiful head as if she would free herself from the fetters of a dark enchantment. With a loud outcry she beholds herself actually in the young man's arms and sees alas! that she has not dreamed it. Wildly with all the strength of horror she pushes him from her, springs up and stands wringing her hands distracted before him, her fluttering hair only half disclosing her frightened countenance. Then she calls him by name in a tone indescribably piercing, painfully questioning, 'Emil!' He in turn, hearing himself called by name, falls at the same moment with a faint sigh swooning to the floor. After a pause he raises himself up, rubs his eyes and looks wonderingly about him. He cannot comprehend how he has come here. The influence of the moon has permitted the poor night wanderer to experience this adventure. When he was completely awake and had come to himself, he stood up and began to think over his situation. Then his eye fell astonished upon Rosalinde, who continued to stare at him speechless and immovable. Shame and anger adorned with a deep glowing color the injured maiden, whose virgin whiteness had been sullied by the strange events of this night. A dark, frightening recollection of what had taken place flashed now like a remote, faded dream into Emil's consciousness. The alluring spirits of the night, which had buzzed around him, now mockingly stripped from him the deceitful mask.

"'Go, go, go!' called Rosalinde finally, who could no longer bear his look. 'Go!' she called and stretched out her hand with a passionate movement toward him, as if she would with it jerk a reeking dagger from her breast. 'Go, go!' she repeated, sobbing and beseeching. Then she hid her aching head with a loud outbreak of tears. Emil slipped away heartbroken and in despair. He was in such a state, when he reached his own room, that he would have put a ball through his head, had there been at that moment a pistol at hand." How Rosalinde then became pregnant and in spite of her resistance toward Emil, still married him to reestablish her honor, how though after the wedding feast two acquaintances of the young husband, whom he had not invited, played him so mischievous a trick that he lost his reason in consequence, that deserves no further rendering.

We find here also as the nucleus of moon walking, when we strip from the foregoing all its mystical setting, the longing to approach the love object and there to be able to indulge oneself without punishment because it is done unconsciously. The literary historian Richard M. Meyer regards it quite correctly: "Theodor Mundt believed that he had emphasized something new in his way of presenting it. 'The influence of the moon had caused the night wanderer to undergo this adventure.'" To be sure Mundt attributes all sorts of mystical-romantic rubbish to the action of the heavenly body.

"DER PRINZ VON HOMBURG," by Heinrich von Kleist.

Heinrich von Kleist also like Ludwig carried night wandering and moon walking into material at hand. We know that Kleist not long before the origin of the "Prinz von Homburg" under Schubert's influence occupied himself very much with the "night side of the natural sciences" and Wukadinovic has made it also apparent that the poet went still deeper, back to one of Schubert's sources, to Reil's "Rhapsodien er die Anwendung der psychischen Kurmethode auf Geisteszerrtungen."[27] There he found a number of features which he then interwove into his drama, although by no means all that he permitted his moonstruck hero to do. The matter of the drama is presumably so well known that I content myself here with giving the mystical setting and the beginning and end of the action.

[27] "Rhapsodies over the Employment of the Psychical Method of Treatment for Mental Disturbances." See Critical Historical Review by W.爛. White, Journ. Nerv. and Ment. Dis., Vol.?3, No.?. [Tr.]

Wearied with a long ride, the Prince von Homburg throws himself down to sleep that he may obtain a little rest before the great battle in which he is about to engage. In the morning when they seek the leader they find him sitting on a bench in the castle park of Fehrbellin, whither the moonlight had enticed the sleep walker. He sits absorbed with bared head and open breast, "Both for himself and his posterity, he dreams the splendid crown of fame to win." Still further, the laurel for this crown he himself must have obtained during the night from the electoral greenhouse. The electress thinks, "As true as I'm alive, this man is ill!" an opinion in which the princess Natalie concurs. "He needs the doctor." But Hohenzollern, his best friend, answers coolly, "He is perfectly well. It is nothing but a mere trick of his mind."

Meanwhile the prince has finished winding the wreath and regards it idly. Then the elector is moved to see how far the former would carry the matter and he takes the laurel wreath out of his hand. "The prince grows red and looks at him. The elector throws his necklace about the wreath and gives it to the princess; the prince stands up roused. The elector withdraws with the princess, who holds up the wreath; the prince follows her with outstretched arms." And now he betrays his inmost wish, "Natalie! my girl, my bride!" In vain the astonished elector, "Go, away with you!" for the prince turns also to him, "Friedrich, my prince, my father!" And then to the electress, "O my mother!" She thinks wonderingly, "Whom is it he thus names?" Yet the prince reaches after the laurel wreath, saying, "Dearest Natalie! Why run away from me?" and really seizes her gloves rather than the wreath. The elector however disappearing with his retinue behind the gates calls to him:

"Away, thou prince of Homburg, get thee back, Naught here for thee, away! The battle's field Will be our meeting place, when't pleases thee! No man obtains such favors in his dreams!"

"The prince remains standing a moment with an expression of wonder before the door, then pondering descends from the terrace, laying his hand, in which he holds the glove, before his forehead, turns as soon as he is below and looks again toward the door." Out of this state the Hohenzollern returning awakens him. At the word "Arthur" the moonstruck prince collapses. "No better could a bullet have been aimed." Afterward of course he makes up some story in regard to his sleep walking, that he had slipped into the garden on account of the great heat. Only the princess's glove recalls to him what has happened in his sleep:

"What is this dream so strange that I have dreamed? For all at once, with gold and silver gleaming, A royal castle flung its portals wide. While from the marble terraced heights above Thronged down to me the happy dancers all; Among them those my love has held most dear. Elector and electress, and-- who is the third? --What name to call her?"

For the name of the princess there is amnesia, as well as for the reason for his moon walking. Then he continues:

"And he, the elector, with brow of mighty Zeus, A wreath of laurel holds within his hand. And pressing close before my very face Plucks from his neck the chain that's pendant there. His hand outstretched he sets it on my locks, My soul meanwhile enkindled high."

Now again the complete forgetting of the loved one's name. He can only say:

"High up, as though to deck the brow of fame, She lifts the wreath, on which the necklace swings, To crown a hero, so her purpose seems. With eager movement I my hands outstretch, No word, mere haste to seize it in my grasp. Down would I sink before her very feet. Yet, as the fragrance over valleys spread Is scattered by the wind's fresh blowing breath, Along the sloping terrace flees the throng. I tread the ramp--unending, far away It stretches up to heaven's very gate, I clutch to right, I clutch to left, and fear No one of all the treasures to secure, No one of all the dear ones to retain. In vain--the castle's door is rudely closed; A flash of brightness from within, then dark, The doors once more swing clatteringly together. And I awaking hold within my hand Naught but a glove, alas! as my reward, Torn from the arm of that sweet dream caught form A glove, ye Gods of power, only this!"

It is evident that there is complete memory of the latter part of his night wandering up to the name of the beloved maiden, although he thinks, "One dumb from birth to name her would be able!" Only once, when he was dreaming by himself, he was on the way toward recollecting the repressed name. He turns even to the Hohenzollern:

"I fain would ask you, my dear friend, The electress, her fair niece, are they still here The lovely princess of the House of Orange, Who lately had arrived at our encampment?"

But he was cut off briefly by his friend, "Eh, what! this long while they've been gone." The same friend had however to explain in detail later, when he appeared before the elector in behalf of the prince condemned to death:

"When I awoke him and his wits he gathered, A flood of joy the memory roused in him; In truth, no sight more touching could you find! At once the whole occurrence, like a dream He spread before me, drawn with finest touch. So vivid, thought he, have I never dreamed.-- And firmer still within him grew belief On him had Heaven a favoring sign bestowed; With all, yes all his inner eye had seen, The maiden, laurel crown and noble jewels, Would God reward him on the battle's day."

We see here plainly that the kernel of the supposed dream belonging to the night wandering is wish fulfilment, desire for glory and the hand of the beloved. It agrees very well with this conception that the prince himself takes the laurel from the gardener's forcing house to wind a wreath of honor for himself. He looks at it with admiring eyes and puts it upon himself, playing the role of being beloved, only the elector and Natalie come in to interfere. The princess and the laurel, also love and fame really hypnotize him and draw him magnetically. The prince follows them both with outstretched arms until the elector and Natalie disappear behind the gates. It seems to me very significant that not long before the creation of this drama a crowning with laurel at the hands of a loved one had actually taken place in the life of the poet and that, as it is now generally admitted, Kleist himself stood as the model of the prince. "Two of the smallest, daintiest hands in Dresden," as Kleist relates, crowned him with laurel at a soir閑 in the house of the Austrian ambassador after the preliminary reading of the "Zerbrochenen Kruges." ("The Broken Pitcher.") These daintiest hands belonged to his beloved Julie Kunze, to whom Dame Rumor said he was engaged. Wukadinovic defines quite correctly the connection of the drama with its autobiographical meaning: "As the poet sees the ideal of love arising next to that of poetic fame, so he grants to the ambitious prince, who exhibits so many of his own traits, a loving woman standing at his side, who rewards him at the close with the wreath."

The matter goes yet much deeper. The prince says of the elector: "Plucks from his neck the chain that's pendant there.... My soul meanwhile enkindled high." The laurel attains a further value for the prince, because the elector binds his own necklace about it. The latter is continually taken by Homburg as the father, to which a number of verses testify. Since the prince unmistakably stands for the poet, it cannot be denied that Kleist had desired the reward not only from the beloved one, but this still more with the express concurrence of the father. In the beginning to be sure he is repulsed by him, "Naught here for thee, away!" and later on account of his disobedience is even condemned to death.[28] He was not only pardoned, however, after he had acknowledged his wrong and recognized the father's judgment as correct, but when he believed his last hour had struck, he was bedecked with the wreath which he desired and on which moreover his elector's chain hangs. Still further, the latter, the father himself, extends the laurel to Natalie and leads the beloved to him. It is beyond question that love is the chief motive of the moon walking of the prince von Homburg, love to a woman as well as a homosexual tendency otherwise authenticated in the case of Kleist. Only it appears here closely amalgamated with desire for fame, something completely unerotic, and with the sexual, as we have found it so far regularly in night wandering and moon walking, quite excluded.

[28] It is significant to compare here the Consul Brutus, who permitted the execution of his sons.

We will attempt to get more light on the last two points. The striving after poetic fame does not remain with our poet within the usual, normal limits but becomes much more a peculiar neurotic characteristic. No less a hope for instance had Heinrich von Kleist than with an unheard of creation to strike at Sophocles, Shakespeare and Goethe and concerning the last named he uttered this audacious sentiment, "I will rend the crown from his brow!" Since he fails to attain this goal in spite of repeated most earnest onslaughts, he rushes away to die upon the battlefield. He writes to his sister, however, "Heaven denies me fame, the greatest of earthly possessions; I fling back to it all else like a self willed child!"

What lay in truth behind that unattainable goal that Kleist tried again and again to carry by force? He himself confesses that it was not the highest poetic art or at least not exclusively so. Otherwise Kleist would have been able to content himself with his so commanding talent and with that which he was able to accomplish with it, like so many other great poets. Let us not forget that he sought to outdo especially the three greatest. Therefore I think, in accordance with all my psychoanalytic experience, that Sophocles, Shakespeare and Goethe are together only father incarnations, that Kleist thus wanted to remove the father from the field. One has a right to definite surmisings on the basis of various works of Kleist, although nothing is known to us of the poet's relations to his parents. The incest motive is one of the chief determining factors of artistic creation, as Rank has outlined in his beautiful book.[29] It is in the first place the desired and striven for incest with the mother herself, in the way of which the father naturally stands. The poet realizes in the freer land of poetry what is impossible in life, by displacing it over a discovered or given material.

[29] Otto Rank, "Das Inzest-Motiv in Dichtung und Sage," 1912, Franz Deuticke.

I discussed in a larger work,[30] previous to Rank's book, how Heinrich von Kleist made the incest phantasies of his childhood the foundation of many poems. So for instance the Marquise von O., assaulted in a fainting fit, is protected from the foe pressing upon her by some one who loves her and will subsequently surely marry her. I need hardly explain that the evil one who will positively force himself upon her is the father, from whom the son defends the mother, that he may subsequently woo her. It is again only the poet himself who sets himself as a youthful ideal god in place of the aging father, as Jupiter descended from his throne renewed in beauty and youth according to his divine power, to visit Alcmene in the form of her spouse Amphitryon. In the "Zerbrochenen Krug" (Broken Pitcher) the judge breaks violently into the room of the beloved one--a typical symbol for one's own father who is also in fact the child's first judge--and is driven out by the rightful lover.

[30] "Heinrich von Kleist. Eine pathographisch-psychologische Studie," 1910, J.燜. Bergmann.

The objection need not be made that the poet has simply held to his pattern. The choice of material betrays the purpose, which frequently remains unconscious. What, we may say, impelled the poet although he wished to translate it wholly, to take up Moliere's Amphitryon, one of his weakest productions too, and then change it in so striking a fashion? Quite unlike the French version, Jupiter becomes for Kleist the advocate with the wife-mother:

"What I now feel for thee, Alcmene dearest, Ah, see! it soars far, far beyond the sun, Which even a husband owes thee. Depart, beloved, flee from this thy spouse, And choose between us, either him or me. I suffer with this shameful interchange, The thought to me is all unbearable, That this vain fellow's been received by thee, Whose cold heart thinks he holds a right o'er thee. Oh! might I now to thee, my sweetest light, A being of another sort appear, Thy conqueror since the art to conquer thee Was taught me by the mighty gods."

In truth Kleist, like every other poet, chose the most of his material in accordance with unconscious wishes, where beyond all else the mother complex presses for poetic expression.

Let us apply once more that which has been so far discovered to the "Prinz von Homburg." This is rendered yet more easy from the fact that the electress is repeatedly designated by the hero as "Mother." His real mother had indeed at her death delivered him over to the friend of her youth with the words: "Be a mother to him when I am no longer here." And the electress had answered in similar strain, "He shall be mine as if my own in birth!" But since on the other hand Natalie also addresses her repeatedly as Mother as she does the elector as Father, so Natalie is Kleist's beloved sister in disguise. The poet would desire the laurel wreath thus from his own sister. Why then the father's acquiescence? If we now appeal to our psychoanalytic experience, this teaches us that regularly the sister incest represents a later form of the older and more serious mother incest. The boy, who first desires the mother, satisfies himself later with the less forbidden and more easily accessible sister. All poets follow very significantly this psychoanalytically established relationship, as Rank[31] has recently convincingly shown. The poets often represent this, that the phantasies and wishes are displaced from the mother to the sister or they are split up between mother and sister, which then makes their origin especially clear.

[31] .

The latter is also the case with Kleist in the "Prinz von Homburg." He takes for the mother he desires, at one time the electress, at another time Natalie, "his girl, his bride."[32] It agrees strikingly also that the prince in the fear of death expects to be saved only by the electress, that is the mother, from the punishment with which the elector father threatens him. So a child who knows no way out for himself, no help any more, flees to his mother. Such an unusual, shocking fear of death on the part of a field officer needs explanation. It is nothing else than the child's fear in face of the stern parent. It is further overdetermined in an infantile way. In the drama the prince for a long time does not believe in the grim seriousness of his position. The elector father will only put him to the test. The sudden transition to frantic fear follows first when the friend informs him that Natalie has sent back the addresses carried by the ambassador, because she is betrothed to the latter. This would have so roused the elector against him. From this time on the prince--and the poet--holds everything as possible and is ready to sacrifice even the hand of the beloved for his life.

[32] It is now plainly understood that the prince can name among the dear ones who appear to him the elector and the electress, that is his mother, but not the third, who is merely a split-off from the latter, at bottom identical

with her.

A second determination likewise is not wanting, which is also infantile. Freud has shown in the "Interpretation of Dreams" that the child does not at all connect the ideas of older people with the words "death" and "to die." He knows neither the terror nor the shuddering fear of the eternal nothingness. To be dead means to him merely to be away, gone away, no longer to be disturbed in his wishes. For his slight experience has already taught him one thing, dead people, as perhaps the grandparents, do not come back. From this it is only a step that the child sometimes wishes death to his father, when the latter disturbs him. Psychoanalysis tells us that this is not perhaps a shocking exception but a matter of everyday occurrence. Such thoughts are touched upon in the "Prinz von Homburg." The false report has come that the elector father has been shot and Natalie laments, "Who will protect us from this world of foes?" Then is the prince ready on the spot to offer his hand to the orphaned girl, also apparently to her mother. A child wish comes to fulfilment, the setting aside of the father who interferes with his plans for the mother. When the man believed to be dead nevertheless returns, he pronounces, as we can understand, the sentence of death upon his treacherous son. Only when the latter had acknowledged the justice of the sentence--I might almost have said, after he had asked forgiveness, is he not only pardoned but more than that recompensed, while now the father voluntarily grants him his wish.

It seems to me significant that Kleist freely introduced into his drama the complete condemnation to death as well as night wandering and moon walking. In the first point he had turned tradition quite to its opposite. In the original the great Friedrich relates that on the triumphant battle field the elector has already forgiven the prince that he had so lightly risked the welfare of the whole state: "If I had judged you according to the stern martial law, you would have forfeited your life. But God forbid that I should sully the brightness of this day by shedding the blood of a prince, who was once the foremost instrument of my victory." Personal reasons, and, as we know from psychoanalysis, these are always infantile reasons, must have been involved when Kleist incorporated this directly into his poetry and yet in so striking a fashion. Some of these reasons I have been able to set forth above.

It is now clear that the apparently asexual desire for fame does not lack its erotic foundation. The desire for fame is so greatly exaggerated in Heinrich von Kleist that he will do no less than tear the laurel from Goethe's forehead, because in his infantile attitude he hopes through an unheard of poetic activity to supplant the father with the mother. After the shipwreck of his masterpiece, the Guiskard material, he longed for death because life had no more value for him, but he finds later in the "Prinz von Homburg" a happier solution. For not only does the mother herself now crown him but does it with the father's affectionate blessing. And the old theme of night wandering and moon walking, that is climbing into bed with the loved one, finds its place here although in an opposite form and under a certain sexual repression. The child does not come to the mother but she to him and places the longed for crown upon his head even with the concurrence of the father. Also the fact that the prince transgresses the elector's commands as the result of his moon walking, to which the prince is subject, must somehow, at least by analogy, have been created from the poet's own breast. Nothing is said about this in regard to Kleist, of whose inner life we know so little. Yet his very great interest in noctambulism and similar "night sides of the human soul," as well as his exceptional understanding of the same, show that he at least must have possessed a disposition toward it. It should be emphasized once more in conclusion that the moon walking in the "Prinz von Homburg" does not lack the infantile sexual root, nor is the corresponding erotic purpose wanting, which we have always found, heretofore, to come to the loved one without being held responsible.

"DAS SUDKIND," by Ludwig Anzengruber.

"Das Sukind" ("The Sin Child") by Anzengruber (in the first volume of his "Dorfg 鎤 ge") tells of an apparently non-sexually colored wandering by moonlight. There a 45-year-old pitch worker, the mother of twelve children, who had all died except the narrator, and for three years a widow, had become pregnant with a "sin child" whose father no one would acknowledge himself. She had always been a discreet woman, and was almost equal to her son in her work, although he at thirty years old was at the height of his manly strength. She had always been as exemplary in love as in her work, a combination, as we know, not rare to find. Having matured early she was with her first child at the age of fifteen and when she was a widow "the people could not wonder enough how long it would be before she showed her age." Not rarely "love" suddenly overcame her and even toward her grown son she could occasionally make quite "God forbidden" eyes. One might almost draw the conclusion from the following circumstance that he also was more deeply dependent on the mother than he might acknowledge to himself. Left alone with her during her confinement, he was not able to look at her but drummed on the window pane and became more and more confused although "God knows, there was no call for it." Then he turned around with his face burning red and said, "You ought to be ashamed, Mother, you ought to be ashamed!" Soon however not only remorse seized him but he began to curse at the folk, who see in the infant not his brother but only the "child of sin." "Do you think for a moment that I would bear a grudge against the little innocent worm? Curse you, anyone who would separate the children of one mother from each other!" After he had lost the love of his youth in earlier years, he had no more interest in women but dwelt with his mother alone on the land which belonged to the family. Later Martin toiled early and late for the illegitimate child Poldl, as if he were its true father, for whom moreover he never might make inquiry.

When Poldl was perhaps sixteen years old, his mother's health began to fail and with her anxiety at approaching death she began to be concerned for her soul, which she, according to human custom, expressed as care for her illegitimate child. He should dedicate himself to the Lord, should become a clergyman, by which he would remain spotless. Martin, with keen insight, thought thus, "That is indeed the easiest way to get rid of one's own sin, to let some one else atone for it" and feared it might go hard with Poldl, hot blooded by inheritance, but he had no effect upon the mother, who was supported by the boy's guardian. Poldl also did not permit himself simply to be talked of by her, but applied himself ever more deeply to his future sacred calling, especially since all the people of the place already paid court to him as if he were even now an ordained clergyman. "Soon he had no other thought than of his future holy office and he might stay or go where he would, for nothing was for him too good or too bad to remind him of it." "He strolled about one entire summer," Martin tells us, "and did not condescend to the least bit of work but when I was out with the farm hands making hay in the meadows or reaping in the field, it very often happened that he rushed unexpectedly out of the bushes and began preaching to them. This seemed quite right to the lazy folk, they would let their work lie and would stand gathered about him and listen devoutly to him and I could not take ill their so excessive piety. The mother thought as they did and found that his absurd preaching there went straight to her heart."

We will stop here a moment. What drove Poldl so to the priestly calling, what made him so intent upon it? We might mention in passing the vanity and the high sense of importance, which is created by the desire in the sixteen year old boy after the most reverend calling. Yet, though I would in no way undervalue his ambition or the satisfaction of a so pleasantly tickled vanity, yet decisive and determining these can scarcely be. Strong motives must govern in order to explain more completely such an impulsion. When Poldl strode over the fields and began to preach, "At that time the Lord Jesus spoke to the disciples?..," then he was indeed not far from conceiving himself as the Holy One and his mother as the Virgin Mary. Jesus had offered himself for the sins of man, as he now for the sin of his mother. According to this it is nothing else than his love to the mother which drives him to the sacred office, in which it is not to be forgotten that such a love, which leads to a thought obsession, is in the light of experience never without the erotic.

This mingling of sensuality and love to the mother, and to an older woman who could be his mother, shows itself still more clearly two years later, when he has a holiday from the seminary for a few days. He finds at home a buxom picture of a woman, a relative on a visit, almost twice as old as he, the very essence of cheeriness and health. "The boy clung closest to her. In spite of his eighteen years he still seemed childish enough and this he turned to account, and 'played the calf with her,'" to use the excellent word of the writer.

Six years later Poldl was appointed to assist an invalid vicar, in whose home a regular vicar's cook kept house with her sixteen year old girl, whom she had from the old vicar. In the same year Poldl's mother was laid to rest and her son appeared at her funeral, where the robust peasant girls and maidens pressed themselves upon him. But he "withdrew shyly from every one of them and gave his hand to no one, as he obligingly might have done. He has always before this appeared like milk and blood," thought Martin, the anxious one, "now he has an unhealthy look, no color, sunken cheeks, and his eyes are deep within, he stares at the ground and cannot bear to have a stranger look at him. It does not please me."

All this is clear and transparent to the physician. In the young man now twenty-four years old the inherited blood began to make itself felt, and at the same time the cook and her daughter let no stimulus be wanting. He suffered under his self restraint, grew pale and hollow and because only his actions remained chaste but not his thought, he could no more look freely upon a woman. When he now preached in the pulpit, he spoke of the devil as the tempter and of all his evil suggestions. He could declare what evil thoughts come to a man and in closing he threatened his flock most earnestly that the devil would carry them all away together. We know well that no sins are more condemned than those which one holds himself capable of committing or which one would himself most gladly commit if only one dared.

The young priest owed it to a great love which he felt for the miller's daughter that he kept himself pure at least in body. So much the more was the vicar's cook intent upon bringing about his downfall through her girl. Then they could again rule at the vicarage, since the old vicar's days were numbered, when Poldl came into the fat living left vacant. It was at the burial of the old priest that Poldl delivered at the grave the funeral oration for the dead, and endeavored to lay the good example which the old man had given upon the hearts of his flock. As he lifted his eyes once and caught those of the miller's Marie-Liese, who was listening so devoutly, not taking her eyes from him, he suddenly remained stuck in the midst of his speech and could find his place in the text again only with difficulty. Was he not able to maintain before her pure glance the fiction of a noble priest, did it come to his consciousness that he was wandering in the same paths on which the other had been most severely wounded? Something of this the miller's daughter seems to have had in mind, for as she later begged his pardon for having confused him by staring at him, at the same time she advised him not to have anything to do with those at the vicarage. The vicar's daughter, who had stolen up unobserved, shook her fist at them both, while her mother drew Poldl later into a corner to give vent to her feelings, "You cannot have the miller's daughter and do not for a moment believe that she would be willing to have you."

On his death bed in the lesser parish, which he held later, he complained to Martin, "I should never have been a priest"--with his inherited passionate blood, in spite of his mother's urging and his love to her. "Martin, you have no idea how hard it is to run caught in a sack; it costs a deal of trouble to keep oneself upright. If one does not twist about one falls into it. The cowl was such a sack for me.... Brother, I have unwittingly fallen into disgrace as a wild beast into a trap, and I am more ashamed of it perhaps than the worst sinner of that which he has done deliberately and maliciously. I would not have stayed in the trap, could everything at first only have remained secret, so that no one would have been afraid to extend a clean hand to me, by which I might have found myself and might again belong to the world and everything. But that the others knew right well and they wanted me for themselves and therefore they have behaved without fear or shame so that soon everything was free and open to all Rodenstein from the forest house at one end to the mill at the other. From that time on I have seen no friendly eye, and the blue, yes, the blue eyes (of the miller's daughter) were always turned defiantly away from me. And because she was unkind to me she became all at once kind to some one whom she formerly could not bear. The folk shook their heads and prophesied little good for her. So the time came when I must come here to this parish. There lay upon me what can soon crush one to the ground, for peace and honor were squandered and those who had won them from me hung like chains upon me and the bit of sunshine that I had had in life I had to leave behind in Rodenstein. When however there was added to this concern for her to whom I owed the bit of happiness, I broke under it and then they took me and brought me here and I let myself be brought."

So had he truly become a child of sin with the feeling of lost purity and a great consciousness of guilt upon his soul. And that he had not merely squandered his own honor and peace but had also dragged the beloved to harm, so that she must have doubts of her purity, this does the rest for him and makes him the willing play ball of the parish folk. From the first day when he took over his new charge, he began to wander in the full moonlight up to the ghostly hour of midnight. At the stroke of twelve he went to the pulpit, over which a bright moonbeam lay, which also lighted up his face as bright as day. With closed eyes he knelt in the pulpit, "his folded hands before him on the upholstered border, the head bowed upon it as if in quiet prayer to collect himself as usual before the sermon. All at once he raised himself, bent forward a little as if the pews were full of people and he wished first to look them over, then he threw his arms to either side and stood there like one who would say, 'Strike me dead, if I have offended you, but I cannot do otherwise!' He did not say this but in a voice as of one speaking in a dream he uttered the words, 'I know of nothing!' And then once more--his hands extended toward heaven and spread open, as if he would show everything to all within or about the church--'I know of nothing!' Afterward he turned and went."

In this classic picture of the brother are some features of a new sort. Above all, sexuality appears only incidentally to play a part, in so far as it awakens the latent tendency to moon walking. Poldl begins to wander at midnight after the miller's daughter is lost to him and he is tortured by anxiety for her future. Otherwise he does what so frequently is done by the moon walker, he carries out the apparently harmless activity of the day as he prays in the church before an imaginary audience. At least he truly imitates the formalities with which prayer begins, though the conclusion does not accord with the beginning. It sounds like a justification before the folk of Rodenstein, who have taken offence at his action, that he stands there in Luther's place as one who cannot do otherwise though one strike him dead. At the same time the repeated outcry at the end, "I know of nothing, I know of nothing!" smacks not only of a denial that he did not know perhaps why Marie had fallen into distress, but suggests the directly infantile. Thus a child insists, when it is reproached, that it has done nothing.

Let us take up again the threads of our narrative. Poldl faded day by day under the pressure of his heavy burden of soul. At last there remained nothing else for him but to let them write to his brother that he lay sick and wished to see him. As Martin entered the sickroom Poldl stretched his lean arms toward him, breathed a heartfelt cry and began to weep aloud like a child. "You are like a father to me, Martin, you are like a father to me!" And from time to time he added, "Forgive me!" Then he stroked Martin's rough hands, "the hands which had toiled for his daily bread when he was a boy." And now he poured forth his confession. He should not have become a priest, then the people of the parish would have remained strangers to him and he perhaps would have succeeded to the Rodenstein mill. His entire concern centered itself about this, that he had not only lost Marie-Liese but was also to blame for the overthrow of her happiness. He related to his brother how the parish folk had apprehended him, so that he was covered with shame, how they all hung about the great bell of Rodenstein until finally the miller's daughter turned from him and to another. After the confession was made Poldl fell asleep contentedly, yet only to wander that very midnight. The invalid was very ill, when Martin talked with him again the next day. And suddenly he began to speak of the days of his childhood and it was remarkable to the brother "how he had remembered the most trivial thing in regard to it and it seemed to me as if he himself often wondered at it in the midst of his speech. Bit by bit thus he took up his life and we talked together of the time when he ran about the sitting-room and the court in his little child's frock, until the time when he went to school, to the seminary, to Rodenstein.... The sun had set when with our prattle we had come to the place where we were, at Weissenhofen. 'That's the end,' I said, 'and there remains nothing else to tell.'--'Yes, yes,' said my brother reflectively, 'that's the end, and there remains nothing more to tell.'" Soon he noticed how truly Martin had spoken in every respect, for the end had come for him now physically. With a blessing on his lips for the newly won brother of his heart, he laid himself down to sleep. "It had become still as a mouse in the room. After perhaps a quarter of an hour I heard him say, 'Yes, yes, were we now together, only you must not hold me so tightly to your breast.' With this he threw himself suddenly over to the right, drew a deep breath, and it was over."

Let us consider once more the circumstances of the moon walking which accompanied this. He begins with this after his removal from Rodenstein and from his heart's beloved. There had preceded the grief over his wasted honor and his forfeited peace, the pain at the loss of the miller's daughter and, which is rather conclusive, the torturing regard for her future, which completely paralyzed his will power. The latter point is somewhat remarkable. For at bottom it was never said that her marriage was unhappy. The people had shaken their heads before it, only, and prophesied nothing good. When Martin fourteen years after the death of his brother meets Marie-Liese at his grave, she has become a handsome woman and has been a widow for eight years but is well poised mentally and lives for her boy. In Poldl's concern the wish must indeed have been father of the thought. If he could not have his treasure, then she should not be happy at the side of another man. Yet apparently this does not refer alone to the miller's daughter. Psychoanalytic experience teaches that where the reaction manifests itself all too strongly this happens because it is not merely a reaction to a present, but above all to a long past experience, which stands behind the other and offers first the original actual tonal background. Only apparently is the effect too strong, if we measure it merely by the actual cause, in truth however the action corresponds to all the causes, that is the new added to the old.

We can say further, if we apply this experience to the poet's narrative, Poldl had not merely lost the miller's daughter forever by entangling himself with the vicar's daughter, but far more another, the one for whom he had entered orders. The mother had said to Martin, "There is only one way, one single way by which my boy can be saved from ruin and I can obtain peace and forgiveness from my sin." This task, to atone for the mother by a holy life, had not prevented him from a passionate love for Marie-Liese or from an intrigue with the pastor's daughter, yet, since he had on the latter's account lost his purity, something else was also laid waste thereby, that which had given peace to him and a purpose to his muddled life, the love for his mother. As he tarried already half in the other world, his last words were, "Yes, yes, were we now together, only you must not hold me so tightly to your breast." This had the mother in her tenderness done to her little boy. We see here the regression to the infantile, to a primitive child libido.

The matter can be followed still further. The walking by moonlight itself did not begin, in spite of every predisposing cause, until Poldl was connected with the new parish and no longer shared the same locality with his beloved. It is not revealed whether the pulpit of the Weissenhofen church looked perhaps in the direction of Rodenstein or not. It seems to me significant that the pastor's daughter crept after Poldl all night long, not perhaps merely the first time, as if she suspected his hidden erotic or feared even that he might go out toward Rodenstein. He must also every midnight establish the fact that, in spite of his sins of the flesh, he considered himself still worthy to be a priest. For the same reason he himself read the mass every day until near the end. Indeed he read this not merely in the daytime but also at midnight when other priests sought rest. And by his behavior in sleep walking it was as if he wished each time anew to justify himself before his Rodenstein parish, and especially before his beloved. The Luther attitude referred to the former, "Though you slay me, I cannot do otherwise!" the outspoken infantile expression, the only words which he actually speaks, "I know of nothing!" is for the latter. Thus a small boy protests his innocence when any one faces him with a misdeed. It was as if he wanted to go back to his beloved, to Marie-Liese, as if to his own mother.

Again we find libidinous and infantile causes as the starting point of moonlight walking and sleep walking. Only the erotic no longer appears so openly as with the other poets but receives a certain disguise. Yet brother

Martin, the philosopher of life, recognizes clearly the kernel of the matter: "So I had also to witness the end with him, as with so many of my brothers and sisters. But I still think today this need not have happened, if the mother had permitted him his life as it would have been lived out freely by himself. First she should not have counted it so great as sin, for otherwise there would have been no pitch worker Poldl in the world. Although she thought of it within herself that it was a sin, she should have so looked upon it that she could have settled it with the Lord God. Ah yes! he had to go about in the cowl, which had become a greater sack than a farmer's jumper and there all the sins of others enter, but if no one shall commit one in his own right, how would one find shelter for all these? If I had only at that time been obstinate about the planning of this thing, I would have foreseen the wrong of it and have known that the mother was an old woman, and with many conscience grows when reason is going to sleep. Faith, honor and peace he would never have squandered, for the farmer's position does not play with so high a stake. Still today the little fellow runs gaily about the yard under my eyes.... Ah, you poor sin child, how wantonly was the joy of living destroyed for you!"

"MACBETH," by Shakespeare.

As I now undertake the analysis of the case of Lady Macbeth, I stand not only before the last but the most difficult portion of my work. Here indeed everything sexual and the erotic itself seem to be quite excluded; and my attempt appears to fail in both directions, in the sexual as well as in the infantile, to apply to Shakespeare's heroine what my psychoanalytically treated cases, as well as all those others from literature have furnished. The poet has devoted no more than one single scene to this entire sleep walking including the grounds for it, and he has said as little of Lady Macbeth's childhood as of her sexual erotic life. Our knowledge of Shakespeare's life is above all so meager, if we turn from the case to the poet himself, that the difficulties tower in our way almost mountain high. The reader will in this case, which presents itself so unfavorably, have to expect neither that certainty nor even that high degree of probability of results, which the earlier examples gave us. Here through no fault of mine all aids to interpretation are wanting. I should consider it as something accomplished if the reader did not say at the close, "The case of Lady Macbeth contradicts all that has been heretofore discovered," as it will appear at first.

We will begin with the literary source for Macbeth, Holinshed's "History of Scotland."[33] Shakespeare confined himself so closely to this that he took over accurately, even to the dialogue, whole scenes into his tragedy. The deviations are for this reason so much the more interesting. In the chronicle Macbeth is simply the tyrant. At the very beginning it is said of him, "he would certainly have been held as the most worthy of rulers, if his nature had not had so strong a tendency to cruelty." His cruelty is frequently emphasized, both at the bier of the dead Macdowald and toward the dwellers in the western isles, who "called him a bloodthirsty tyrant and the cruel murderer of those to whom the king's grace had granted their lives." Finally also in the camp of the Danes when they were overcome "he wrought such havoc upon all sides without the least resistance that it was terrible to look upon." A change seems however to have taken place in his character when, after the murder of Duncan, he had seized the kingdom for himself. "He began to reform the laws and to root out all the irregularities and abuses in the administration." He freed the land for many years from all robbers, guarded most carefully the church and clergy, and, to put it briefly, was looked upon as the defender and shield of everything blameless. He established also many good laws and ruled the kingdom for ten years with the greatest wisdom and justice.

[33] I cite this according to "Die Quellen des Shakespeare," by Karl Simrock, 2d edition, 1870.

"This apparent equity and zeal for all that is best was however merely hypocrisy; he wished only to win the favor of the people. Tyrants are always distrustful, they are always afraid that others will rob them of their power by the same unrighteous means by which they themselves have succeeded. As soon as Macbeth discovered any plans against himself, he no longer concealed his intentions but practised and permitted every kind of cruelty." At first the words of the three sisters of fate lay always in his thoughts. In order to attain to what they had prophesied he was willing to have Banquo and his son murdered. Yet the murderers hired for the purpose killed only the former while Fleance succeeded in escaping. "Luck seems to have deserted Macbeth after the murder of Banquo. None of his undertakings were successful, every one feared for his life and scarcely dared appear before the king. He feared every one and every one feared him, so that he was always seeking opportunity for the execution of suspected persons. His distrust and his cruelty increased day by day, his bloodthirstiness was not to be appeased.... He gave himself over recklessly to his natural ferocity, oppressed his subjects even to the poorest and permitted himself every shameful deed." Shakespeare has represented the rest fairly truly according to Holinshed, only that in actuality this lasted for seven years, until Macbeth fell at the hands of Macduff.

It is also worthy of note what Holinshed has made the ground of the murder of Duncan. There preceded in the chronicle the promise of the three witches, further Malcolm's appointment as prince of Cumberland and, as a result of this, succession to the kingdom. Now Malcolm could "ascend the throne directly after his father's death, while in the old laws it was provided that the nearest relative would be placed upon the throne, if, at the death of his predecessor, the prince who was called to the succession was not yet capable of ruling." This latter had happened to Macbeth, Duncan's cousin. "Then began Macbeth, from whom by this arrangement of the king all hope of the throne was taken, to consider the means whereby he could seize the crown by force for himself. For he believed that Duncan had done him a great wrong, when he named his infant son as successor to his throne and had so annulled all other claims. Moreover the words of the witches encouraged him to his purpose. But foremost of all his wife, a proud and haughty woman, who longed with most burning desire after the name of queen, would not desist until she had strengthened him to the uttermost in his intention." This last sentence is the chronicler's only notice of Lady Macbeth.

We can now measure what Shakespeare has contributed himself to her character as well as to that of her husband. At first the absolute cruelty, which with Holinshed was the chief trait of his character, is wanting in Macbeth, and therefore ambition is mentioned first. Macbeth becomes the tyrant wading in blood first after the murder of Duncan and then more from a necessity to defend himself. His own wife characterizes best the earlier hero:

"Yet I do fear thy nature; It is too full o' the milk of human kindness, To catch the nearest way; Thou would'st be great; Art not without ambition; but without The illness should attend it. What thou would'st highly That would'st thou holily, would'st not play false, And yet would'st wrongly win: thou'd'st have, great Glamis, That which cries, Thus thou must do, if thou have it; And that which rather thou dost fear to do, Than wishest should be undone."

Yet Macbeth at bottom dared not murder the king, he only toyed with the thought. He must be instigated from without, if the deed is not to be put off until the Greek calends. Lady Macbeth from the very beginning feels it her task to strengthen her laggard and doubting husband in his ambition. This Shakespeare had already found in Holinshed. As the chronicle has pictured it: "Still more did his wife urge him on to attack the king, for she was exorbitantly ambitious and burned with an inextinguishable desire to bear the name of queen."[34] While she thus incited her husband, she fulfilled yet more the longing of her own heart:

"Hie thee hither, That I may pour my spirits in thine ear; And chastise with the valour of my tongue All that impedes thee from the golden round."

[34] The words of Holinshed's chronicle.

She summons herself also to the task, calls the evil spirits of the air to her aid and will become a man, since her husband is no man:

"Come, come, you spirits That tend on mortal thoughts, unsex me here; And fill me, from the crown to the toe, top-full Of direst cruelty! Make thick my blood, Stop up the access and passage to remorse; That no compunctious visitings of nature Shake my fell purpose, nor keep peace between The effect and it! Come to my woman's breasts, And take my milk for gall, you murd'ring ministers!"

When Macbeth announces, "Duncan comes here to-night," she asks sinisterly, "And when goes hence?"--Macbeth: "To-morrow--as he purposes."--Lady Macbeth:

"O, never Shall sun that morrow see! . . . . He that's coming Must be provided for; and you shall put This night's great business into my despatch; Which shall to all our nights and days to come Give solely sovereign sway and masterdom."

It may be seen that the really cruel one is here first Lady Macbeth and not her husband. He on the contrary must always torture himself with scruples and doubts. He constantly holds before himself the outward results of his deed, brings everything together which should protect Duncan from his dagger and can only say in regard to the opposite course:

"I have no spur To prick the sides of my intent, but only Vaulting ambition, which o'er-leaps itself, And falls on the other."

And he explains to his wife, "We will proceed no further in this business." Then must Lady Macbeth rebuke him as a coward, no longer trust his love, if he, when time and place so wait upon him, retract from his purpose. She lays on the strongest accent, yes, uses the "word of fury":

"I have given suck; and know How tender 'tis to love the babe that milks me; I would, while it was smiling in my face, Have plucked my nipple from his boneless gums, And dashed the brains out, had I so sworn, as you Have done to this."--

and finally develops the entire plan and promises her assistance, before she can persuade her husband to the murder.

She has stupefied the two chamberlains, upon whom the guilt shall be rolled, with spiced wine and drunk herself full of courage for the deed, as so many criminals.

"That which hath made them drunk, hath made me bold; What hath quenched them, hath given me fire."

Then she hears Macbeth within at his gruesome work uttering a terrified question, and continues:

"Alack! I am afraid they have awaked, And 'tis not done:--the attempt, and not the deed, Confounds us;--Hark!--I laid their daggers ready, He could not miss them.--Had he not resembled My father as he slept, I had done't."

Then her husband appears with the daggers. As he looks at his bloody hands a cry is wrung from him, "This is a sorry sight." Yet the Lady repulses him harshly, "A foolish thought, to say a sorry sight."

Macbeth:

"Methought, I heard a voice cry, Sleep no more! Macbeth doth murder sleep . . . . . And therefore ... Macbeth shall sleep no more!"

Lady Macbeth quiets him but he weakens his high courage by brooding over the deed.

"Go, get some water, And wash this filthy witness from your hand.-- Why did you bring these daggers from the place? They must lie there. Go, carry them; and smear The sleepy grooms with blood."

Then however as her husband refuses to look again upon his deed Lady Macbeth herself seizes the daggers:

"The sleeping and the dead Are but as pictures; 'tis the eye of childhood, That fears a painted devil. If he do bleed, I'll gild the faces of the grooms withal."

Macbeth (alone):

"Will all great Neptune's ocean wash this blood Clean from my hand? No; this my hand will rather The multitudinous seas incarnadine, Making the green one red."

Lady Macbeth (returning):

"My hands are of your colour; but I shame To wear a heart so white . . . . retire we to our chamber: A little water clears us of this deed; How easy is it then! Your constancy Hath left you unattended."

But the horrid deed has not brought the expected good fortune. After Duncan's murder Macbeth finds no rest and no sleep: "To be thus, is nothing; But to be safely thus." So he first considers removing Banquo and his son. But Lady Macbeth is little content:

"Nought's had, all's spent, Where our desire is got without content; 'Tis safer to be that which we destroy, Than, by destruction, dwell in doubtful joy."

Then comes her husband. All night he has been so shaken with terrible dreams that he would rather be in Duncan's place, "Than on the torture of the mind to lie, In restless ecstasy." Lady Macbeth tries here to comfort him with the only tender impulse in the drama:

"Come on; Gentle my lord, sleek o'er your rugged looks; Be bright and jovial 'mong your guests to-night."[35]

Macbeth promises to do as she asks and charges her to treat Banquo especially with distinction. Nor does he conceal from her what now tortures him most, "Dear wife, Thou knowest that Banquo, and his Fleance, lives." And immediately the Lady is her old self: "But in them nature's copy's not eterne." Though Lady Macbeth is represented as at once prepared for a second murder, Macbeth has now no more need of her: "Be innocent of the knowledge, dearest chuck, Till thou applaud the deed."

[35] One notes the emptiness of this passage. She could scarcely have said much less, if she wished to comfort him. And yet this passage is always quoted by those authors who accept love on the part of Lady Macbeth for her husband as the driving motive for her action. Indeed, Friedrich Theodor Vischer himself does not shrink from an interpolation and translates the passage: Lady Macbeth ("caressingly")--"Come, come, my noble lord, remove thy wrinkles, smooth thy gloomy brow, be jovial this evening, well-disposed toward thy guests." And although the original English text contains no word for "caressingly," yet Vischer gives this commentary: "His wife's answer to him must be spoken on the stage with an altogether tender accent. She embraces him and strokes his forehead." (Shakespeare-Vortr 鋄 e, Vol.?, pp.?6, 102.)

Yet, although he shrinks back no longer from any sort of evil deed, he does so before the horrible pictures of his phantasies, the hallucinations of his unconscious. Here is where Shakespeare's genius enters. The Macbeth of the Chronicle commits throughout all his acts of horror apparently in cold blood. At least nothing to the contrary is reported. With Shakespeare on the other hand Macbeth, who is represented in the beginning as more ambitious than cruel, is pathologically tainted. From his youth on he suffered from frequent visions, which, for example, caused him to see before Duncan's murder an imaginary dagger. This "strange infirmity, which is nothing To those that know me," comes to light most vividly on the appearance of Banquo's ghost at the banquet. Lady Macbeth must use all her presence of mind to save at least the outward appearance. With friendly exhortation, yet with grim reproof and scornful word, she attempts to bring her husband to himself. In this last scene, when she interposes in Macbeth's behavior, she stands completely at the height. Not until the guests have departed does she grow slack in her replies. In truth neither her husband's resolution to wade on in blood nor his word that strange things haunt his brain can draw from her more than the response, "You lack the season of all natures, sleep." It seems as if she had collapsed exhausted after her tremendous psychical effort.

Shakespeare has in strange fashion told us nothing of what goes on further in her soul, though he overmotivates everything else, even devotes whole scenes to this one purpose. We first see her again in the last act in the famous sleep walking scene. She begins to walk in her sleep, falls ill with it one might well say, just on that day when Macbeth goes to war. Her lady in waiting saw her from this day on, at night, "rise from her bed, throw her nightgown upon her, unlock her closet, take forth paper, fold it, write upon it, read it, afterwards seal it, and again return to bed; yet all this while in a most fast sleep."--"A great perturbation in nature! to receive at once the benefit of sleep, and do the effects of watching," the evidently keen sighted physician thinks. He soon has the opportunity to observe the Lady's sleep walking for himself. She comes, in her hand a lighted candle, which at her express command must be always burning near her bed. Her eyes are open as she walks, but their sense is shut. Then she rubs her hands together as if to wash them, which she does according to the statement of the lady in waiting, often continuously for a quarter of an hour.

Now they hear her speaking: "Yet here's a spot. Out damned spot! out, I say!--One, two, why, then 'tis time to do't.--Hell is murky!--Fie, my lord! a soldier, and afear'd? What need we fear who knows it, when none can call our power to account?--Yet who would have thought the old man to have had so much blood in him?--The Thane of Fife had a wife; Where is she now?--What, will these hands ne'er be clean?--No more o' that, my lord, no more o' that; you mar all with this starting.--Here's the smell of the blood still; all the perfumes of Arabia will not sweeten this little hand. Oh! oh! oh!--Wash your hands, put on your nightgown; look not so pale;--I tell you yet again, Banquo's buried; he cannot come out of his grave.--To bed, to bed; there's knocking at the gate. Come, come, come, come, give me your hand. What's done cannot be undone. To bed, to bed, to bed." After such appearances she always in fact goes promptly to bed. The physician who observes her pronounces his opinion: "This disease is beyond my practice. Yet have I known those which have walked in their sleep, who have died holily in their beds." Here however there seems to be something different:

"Foul whisperings are abroad; unnatural deeds Do breed unnatural troubles."

And then as if he were a psychoanalyst:

"Infected minds To their deaf pillows will discharge their secrets. More needs she the divine, than the physician.-- God, God forgive us all! Look after her; Remove from her the means of all annoyance, And still keep eyes upon her."

Also he answers Macbeth, who inquires after the condition of the patient.

"Not so sick, my lord, As she is troubled with thick-coming fancies, That keep her from her rest.... . . . . Therein the patient Must minister to himself."

Yet as the king's star declines neither the doctor's foresight nor his skill prevents Lady Macbeth, the "diabolical queen" from laying hands upon herself.

This case of sleep walking, if we consider it, seems first to correspond entirely to the popular view, that the wanderer carries over to the nighttime the activities of the day, or to speak more correctly, of the most important day of the last month. We saw in the first act how she reproaches Macbeth for his cowardice, encourages him and controls his actions. Only in two points, very significant ones to be sure, does it appear that she has now taken over her husband's role upon herself; in the disturbance of her sleep and the concern for the blood upon her hands. How had she rebuffed Macbeth when he had called out in regard to his bloody hands, "This is a sorry sight!" It was only a foolish thought. "Go get some water, And wash this filthy witness from your hand." But Macbeth was not to be shaken, the entire ocean would not suffice. Rather would the king's blood, which he had shed, change its green to glowing red. Yet when Lady Macbeth completes his work for him, she remarks lightly, "My hands are of your color; but I shame To wear a heart so white.... A little water clears us of this deed." In her sleep walking itself she encourages her husband, "Wash your hands, put on your nightgown." She seeks however in vain in this very sleep walking to wipe the stains from her hands, they smell always of blood and not all the perfumes of Arabia will sweeten her hands. Must not the inner meaning of all her sleep walking lie exactly in these two points, in which she has so completely turned about?

It must be observed that in the tragedy as in the previously related tale of the "Sin Child" the sleep walking does not begin in childhood nor in puberty, but in both instances in somewhat more mature years, and, what is significant, as an illness, more precisely a psychic illness. The sin child fell ill because he had lost his pure beloved one, who had taken the place of his mother, the original love object of his earliest childhood; and Lady Macbeth, who had herself become queen through a murder, falls ill just at that moment when her lord must go to the battlefield to defend his life and his crown. For not without reason the fate of Macduff's wife, who was slain when her husband had gone from her, occurs to her also when she, while wandering, speaks of the much blood which Duncan had. Therefore it seems likely, and is in fact generally believed, that Lady Macbeth becomes ill because of her anxiety for life and kingdom. Only the facts do not strictly agree with this. In the first place her husband's campaign is by no means unpromising. On the contrary he has heard from the witches that his end would be bound with apparently unfulfillable conditions, so unfulfillable that the prophecy at once frees him from all fear.

Having hidden nothing from the "partner of his greatness" he would scarcely conceal the promise of the witches, which increased his confidence to the uttermost. Besides it cannot be fear and anxiety which brings on her night wandering. Another current explanation also seems to me to have little ground. As Brandes has recently interpreted it, "The sleep walking scene shows in the most remarkable fashion how the pricking of an evil conscience, when it is dulled by day, is more keen at night and robs the guilty one of sleep and health." Now severe pangs of conscience may well disturb sleep, but they would hardly create sleep walking. Criminals are hardly noctambulists. Macbeth himself is an example how far stings of conscience and remorse can lead a sensitive man. He has no more rest after he has murdered the king and Banquo, yet he does not become a sleep walker. There must be another cause here which precipitates Lady Macbeth's sleep walking.

We will first examine the relation of husband and wife to one another in order to trace out this mystery. The character of Lady Macbeth has caused many a one in Germany to rack his brains since the time of Tieck. Up till that time she passed simply as Megaera, as an "arch witch," as Goethe calls her. This opinion prevailed not only in Germany but in the English motherland too. But this view went against the grain with the German spirit. Therefore Ludwig Tieck first looked upon Lady Macbeth as a tender, loving wife. From this time on there arose critics and even poets, who in the same way wished to wash her clean. I will cite the two most important, Friedrich Theodor Vischer and Rudolf Hans Bartsch. The former, of whom I explained earlier, that he did not hesitate to make an interpolation to prove his point, sums up his judgment in the following sentences: "It is not ambition alone that moves her, but love which would see her lord become great" (p. 78). And in a second place, "She loved her husband and had sacrificed her conscience more for him than for herself" (p. 124). R. H. Bartsch goes much further in his romance, "Elisabeth Kitt." Wigram says to the heroine, "Do you not feel how she (Lady Macbeth) before everything that she says cannot hitch horses enough to carry her slow and immovable lord along?" In the sleep walking scene "the utter crushing of this poor, overburdened heart burst forth in the torture of the dream wandering." At the close he pronounces his opinion: "If there is a poor weak woman upon earth, so it is this arch enchantress, who loves her husband so much that she has in admirable fashion studied all his faults and weaknesses that she may cover over the deficiencies with her trembling body. Seek the wife in her role!"

What truth is there in these viewpoints? The poet himself has been dead for three hundred years and has left behind him not a syllable concerning Lady Macbeth except in the text of the tragedy. Therefore according to my opinion nothing remains but to keep to this. At the most we can draw upon Holinshed's chronicle, which Shakespeare so frequently followed literally. According to this Lady Macbeth was extravagantly ambitious and when she continually urged Macbeth to murder Duncan, this was only because she "burned with an unquenchable desire to bear the name of queen." There is never a syllable of a feeling of love for her husband, or that she desired the crown only for his sake. This objection might be made here, that as Shakespeare has often gone beyond his source, as in creating the sleep walking scene without a model for it, so he might just as well have given characters to Lady Macbeth of which the source said nothing. Certainly that would be a priori conceivable. Only that must appear clearly from the text of the tragedy. Yet what does this say? Carefully as I have read its lines, I have not been able to find a single, actual uninterpolated word of love from Lady Macbeth. That is of double significance from the poet of "Romeo and Juliet." He who could give such language to love would not have completely denied it in "Macbeth," if Lady Macbeth was to have been a loving wife. One can find everything in her words, warning, entreaty and adjuration, upbraidings and threatenings, anger, yes, almost abuse, yet not one natural note of love.

This has a so much harsher effect since her husband approaches her usually as an actual lover, or more accurately stated up to the murder of Banquo. She is warm only where it concerns the attainment of her goal; it is her ambition which demands satisfaction. She is always to her husband "my dearest partner of my greatness" as he once appropriately writes her. It is not to be considered that Shakespeare, who always overmotivates his situations, should have at the height of his power so obscured from recognition all the love impulses, which would have seemed to be decisive for her whole character. The truth is simply that Lady Macbeth is no loving wife, but merely greedy of fame, as already represented in the Chronicle. I suspect that the authors who all the way through see in her the loving spouse are expressing their own complexes, their own unconscious wishes. Such an one as Bartsch for example cannot think otherwise of a woman than as unfolding lovingly to the man.

Lady Macbeth makes upon me, in her relation toward her frequently wooing husband as it were, the impression of a natura frigida, that is a sexually cold woman. If one takes her own frightful word for it, that she could tear the breast from her own sucking child and dash its brains out, then the mother love seems never to have been strong within her, but rather whatever feeling she has possessed has been changed to passionate ambition. Now psychoanalytic experience teaches that when a woman remains sexually cold toward a sympathetic and potent man, this goes back to an early sealing up of affect with a forbidden, because an incest object. Such women have almost always from their tenderest infancy on loved father or brother above all and never through all their lives freed themselves from this early loved object. Though at puberty compelled to cut them off as sexual objects, yet they have held fast to them in the unconscious and become incapable of transferring to another man. It is possible also in the case of Lady Macbeth to think of such an indissoluble bond. Moreover certain features in the sleep walking scene seem to speak directly of a repressed sexual life.

Lady Macbeth wanders at night, since her husband has left her and marital intercourse has been broken off.[36] In her hand is a lighted candle, which according to her express command must burn near her bed, and only now for the first time, otherwise the lady in waiting would not have laid such stress upon the fact. The candle in her hand, that is a feature which up till now we have met in none of our cases, but which, as a glance into literature teaches me, is by no means infrequently found with sleep walkers. It can hardly be considered a mere accident that Shakespeare discovered just this characteristic, which is really atypical. One would be much more inclined to suspect in it a secret, hidden meaning. Then at once a connection forces itself. We know from the infantile history of so many people that a tenderly solicitous parent, the father or the mother, likes to convince himself or herself, with a candle in the hand, that the child is asleep.[37] Then we would have on one side a motive for sleep walking in general, that one is playing the part of the loving parent, as on the other hand a motive for the lighted candle. The latter has however a symbolic sexual sense which is quite typical and is repeatedly and regularly found. The burning candle always stands for one thing and signifies in dreams as in fairy tales, folklore, and sagas without exception the same thing, an erect phallus. Now it becomes clear why Lady Macbeth, after her husband had gone to the war, has a lighted candle always burning near her bed, and why then she wanders around like a ghost with it at night.

[36] This is not without significance as a direct precipitating cause, although naturally not the true source of her night wandering.

[37] A second still more important motivation for the nightly visit I will discuss later.

The conclusion of the words she utters during her sleep walking contains a second unmistakably sexual relationship. Here she repeats not less than five times the demand upon her husband, "To bed," while in the corresponding murder scene (II, 2) it simply reads, "Retire we to our chamber; A little water clears us of this deed." The further repetition, "Come, come, come, come, give me your hand," sounds again infantile through and through. So one speaks to a child, scarcely to an adult. It seems as if she takes the father or the mother by the hand and bids them go to bed. One recognizes already in this passage that this atypical sleep walking of Lady Macbeth also leads naturally into the sexual and the infantile.

It will not be difficult to determine now toward whom the repressed, because strongly forbidden, sexual wishes of Lady Macbeth are directed. Who else could it be but her own father, the original love object of every little girl; what other person of her childhood, who later becomes an unsuitable sexual object, but yet hinders for all the future the transference of love over to the husband? This is the one who summons her to walk in her sleep, the lighted candle in her hand. It is quite an everyday experience, which holds for everyone, for the well as for every one who later becomes ill, that in reality the first love, which bears quite clearly features of sense pleasure, belongs to the earliest years of childhood, and that its objects are none other than the child's own parents and in the second place the brothers and sisters. Here the polar attraction of the sexes holds in the relation of the elder to the younger and vice versa, that is the attraction of the man to the woman and the woman to the man. It is "a natural tendency," says Freud[38] in the "Interpretation of Dreams," "for the father to indulge the little daughter, and for the mother to take the part of the sons, while both work earnestly for the education of the little ones when the magic of sex does not prejudice their judgment. The child is very well aware of any partiality, and resists that member of the parental couple who discourages it.... Thus the child obeys its own sexual impulse, and at the same time reinforces the feeling which proceeds from the parents, if it makes a selection among the parents that corresponds to theirs."

[38] Freud: The Interpretation of Dreams, translated by A.爛. Brill. The Macmillan Company, London, New York, 4th edition, p.?18.

We will stop here at two factors which will occupy us again later, the being in love with the parent of the opposite sex, and then the resistance against the one of the same sex. Corresponding to the love, every child in the period of innocence wants to "marry" the former. I recall what a colleague told me of a dialogue between him and his little five year old daughter. She began, "I want to get married."--"To whom?"--"To you, Papa."--"I already have a wife."--"Then you would have two wives."--"That won't do."--"Very well, then I will choose a man who is as nice as you." And Freud relates (p. 219), "An eight year old girl of my acquaintance, when her mother is called from the table, takes advantage of the opportunity to proclaim herself her successor. 'Now I shall be Mamma; Charles, do you want some more vegetables? Have some, I beg you,' and so on. A particularly gifted and vivacious girl, not yet four years old, ... says outright: 'Now mother can go away; then father must marry me and I shall be his wife.'"

We will add just one more little experience to give us a broader point of view. The interpretation of dreams, fairy tales and myths teaches us regularly that the phantasies of the child, like those of all peoples in their period, identify father with king or emperor. Naturally then the father's wife becomes the queen. This fact of experience, which is always to be substantiated, can be applied to Lady Macbeth and makes her ambition at once transparent to us. I affirmed above that her lack of sexual feeling toward her husband had its origin in the fact that she had loved her father too much and could not therefore free herself from him. Her sexuality had transformed itself into ambition and that, the ambition to be queen,[39] in other words, the father's wife. So could she hold fast to the infantile ideal and realize the forbidden incest. The intensity with which she pursues the ambition of her life is explained then by the glowing intensity of her sexual wishes.

[39] Holinshed's chronicle lays emphasis upon this: "She ... burned with an inextinguishable desire to bear the name of queen."

With Shakespeare also king and father come together. A remark of Lady Macbeth shows that when she addresses herself to the murder of Duncan. "Had he not resembled my father as he slept, I had done't." This physical likeness signifies identity of individuals, as we know from many analogous examples. The king therefore resembles the father because he stands for her parent. Still one more point may be well explained from her father complex. The Chronicle speaks of the overweening ambition of Lady Macbeth. Now we know from neuropsychology that burning ambition in later years represents a reaction formation to infantile bed wetting. It is the rule with such children that they are placed upon the chamber at night by father or mother. Thus we comprehend from another side, with the so frequent identification with beloved persons, precisely why the lady wanders at night with a candle in her hand. Here again appears plainly the return to the infantile erotic.

Now for the grounds of her collapse. As long as Lady Macbeth is fighting only for the childish goal, she is an unshakeable rock amid the storms of danger. She shrinks from no wrong and no crime that she may be queen at her husband's side. But she must gradually perceive that her husband will never win satisfaction, he will never recover from the king-father murder, her hopes will never be fulfilled and she will never live in quiet satisfaction at the side of her father. Then her power of endurance gives way until her very soul fails utterly. As she says on the occasion of the first disappointment after Duncan's death:

"Nought's had, all's spent, Where our desire is got without content; 'Tis safer to be that which we destroy, Than, by destruction, dwell in doubtful joy."

Now the unconscious, hitherto successfully repressed, avenges itself, now conscience awakes and as the husband leaves her completely alone she begins to wander, that is to seek to return to the infantile ideal. In her wandering she herself plays the role of father, who once approached her with the lighted candle and then called to her, "Come, come, come, come, give me your hand!" and bade her go to bed.

Why however does not the ruthless Macbeth live down the murder of the king as he does in the history? I believe that we must here go still further back than to the Chronicle, even to the creator of the tragedy himself. There is a certain important crisis in Shakespeare's life, where according to the biography by George Brandes "cheerfulness, the very joy of life, was extinguished in his soul. Heavy clouds gathered over his horizon, we now do not know just what their source. Gnawing griefs and disappointments gathered within him. We see his melancholy grow and extend itself; we can observe the changing effects of this melancholy without clearly recognizing its cause. Only we feel this, that the scene of action which he sees with the inner eye of the soul has now become as black as the external scene of which he makes use. A veil of phantasy has sunk down over both. He writes no more comedies but puts a succession of dark tragedies upon the stage, which lately re 惟 hoed to the laughter of his Rosalinds and Beatrices."

This crisis came in the year 1601, when the earl of Essex and Lord Southampton, Shakespeare's special patron, were condemned to death because of treason against the life of the king. According to Brandes the depression over their fate must have been one of the original causes for the poet's beginning melancholy. Perhaps the death of Shakespeare's father, which followed some months later, made a more lasting impression with all the memories which it recalled. The dramas which the poet published about that time, Julius Caesar, Hamlet and Macbeth, have a common theme, they all revolve about a father murder. In "Julius Caesar," Brutus murders his fatherly friend, his mother's beloved ("And thou too, my son Brutus?"). Hamlet comes to shipwreck in his undertaking to avenge upon his uncle the father's murder, because the uncle, as Freud explains in his "Interpretation of Dreams," had at bottom done nothing else than Hamlet had wished in his childhood but had not had the self confidence to carry out. And Macbeth in the last analysis is ruined by the king and father murder, the results of which he can never overcome. We may consider this theme of the father murder, always presented in some new form, in the light of its direct precipitating causes, the actual death of Shakespeare's father and Southampton's treason against the ruling power of the state. It is not difficult to accept that at that time the infantile death wishes against his father were newly awakened in our poet himself and were then projected externally in a series of powerful dramas.

Perhaps the reader, who has followed me more or less up to this point, will stop here indignant: "How could any one maintain that a genius like Shakespeare could have wished to murder his father, even if only in the phantasies of childhood?" I can only reply to this apparently justified indignation that the assumption I here make concerning Shakespeare is fundamentally and universally human and is true with every male child. We go for proof to what we have earlier discovered, that the first inclination of every child, also already erotically colored, belongs to the parent of the opposite sex, the love of the girl to the father, the leaning of the boy to his mother, while the child sets himself against the parent of the same sex, who may be only justly concerned in his education without over indulging him. The child would be most delighted to "marry" the tender parent, as we heard above, and therefore feels that the other parent stands in the way as a disturbing rival. "If the little boy," says Freud in the "Interpretation of Dreams,"[40] "is allowed to sleep at his mother's side whenever his father goes on a journey, and if after his father's return he must go back to the nursery to a person whom he likes far less, the wish may be easily actuated that his father may always be absent, in order that he may keep his place next to his dear, beautiful mamma; and the father's death is obviously a means for the attainment of this wish; for the child's experience has taught him that 'dead' folks, like grandpa, for example, are always absent; they never return."

[40] Freud, p.?19.

Yet how does the child reach such a depth of depravity as to wish his parents dead? We may answer "that the childish idea of 'being dead' has little else but the words in common with our own. The child knows nothing of the horrors of decay, of shivering in the cold grave, of the terror of the infinite Nothing.... Fear of death is strange to the child, therefore it plays with the horrible word.... Being dead means for the child, which has been spared the scenes of suffering previous to dying, the same as 'being gone,' not disturbing the survivors any more. The child does not distinguish the manner and means by which this absence is brought about, whether by traveling, estrangement or death.... If, then, the child has motives for wishing the absence of another child, every restraint is lacking which would prevent it from clothing this wish in the form that the child may die."[41] It may be conjectured, if we apply this to Shakespeare, that also this greatest of all dramatists repeatedly during his childhood wished his father dead and that this appeared in consciousness agitating him afresh at the actual decease of the father and impelled him to those dramas which had the father murder as their theme. Moreover the father's calling, for he was not only a tanner but also a butcher, who stuck animals with a knife, may have influenced the form of his death wishes as well as of their later reappearances in the great dramas.

[41] Freud, I pp.?15, 216.

The evil thoughts against the father in the child psyche by no means exclude the fact that at the same time there are present with them tender impulses, feelings of warmest love. This is indeed the rule according to all experience and can be proved also with Shakespeare. This other side of his childish impulse leads for example to the powerful ambition which we find as a chief characteristic of Macbeth and Lady Macbeth, as in truth of the poet himself. We know that when the latter was a boy his father became bankrupt. He had not only lost everything which he himself possessed, his wife's dowry and his position as alderman, but was also so deeply in debt at this time that he had to guard himself against arrest. Once more I let Brandes express it: "The object of Shakespeare's desire was not in the first place either the calling of a poet or fame as an actor, but wealth and that chiefly as a means for social advance. He took very much to heart his father's decline in material fortune and official respect. He held passionately from his youth up to the purpose to reestablish the name and the position of his family.... His father had not dared to go along the streets, fearing to be arrested for debt. He himself as a young man had been whipped at the command of the landowner and thrown into jail. The small town which had been the witness of these humiliations should be witness of the restoration of his honor. Where he had been spoken of as the actor and playwright of doubtful fame, there would he be seen again as the honored possessor of house and land. There and elsewhere should the people, who had counted him among the proletariat, learn to know him as a gentleman, that is as a member of the lesser nobility.... In the year 1596 his father, apparently at his instigation and with his support, entered a petition at Heralds College for the bestowal of a coat of arms. The granting of the coat of arms signified the ceremonial entry into the gentry." The ambition of the small child is to become as great as the father, and so later that of the man is to exalt the father himself, to make him king. One sees how close and how very personal the theme of ambition was to Shakespeare.

Before I go on to analyze further what the poet has woven into his treatment of "Macbeth" from his own purely personal experience, we must first consider a technical factor which is common to all dramatists. It has been discovered that Shakespeare projected his own complexes into his tragedies, complexes which are in no way simple, but which show, for example, close to the hatred even as great a love as well as other contrary elements. He is fond of separating his dramatic projection into two personalities wherever his feeling is an ambivalent one, these two forms standing in contrast to one another. He splits his ego into two persons, each of which corresponds to only one single emotional impulse. That is a discovery which of course was not made for the first time by psychoanalysis. Minor, for instance, writes in his book on Schiller: "Only in conjunction with Carlos does Posa represent Schiller's whole nature, the wild passion of the one is the expression of the sensual side, the noble exaltation of the other the stoical side of his nature.... Schiller has not drawn this figure from external nature; it has not come to him from without but he has taken it deep from his inner being." Otto Ludwig expresses himself similarly: "Goethe often separates a man into two poetic forms, Faust-Mephisto, Clavigo-Carlos."

It is plainly to be seen, if we apply our recognition of this fact to Shakespeare, that he has projected his ego affect into Macbeth as well as his wife, which gives numerous advantages. So far we have considered Lady Macbeth merely as a complete dramatic character, which she is first of all. Besides this nevertheless she surely corresponds to a splitting of Shakespeare's affect, for the poet incorporates in her his instincts for ruthless ambition. He has worked over the character already given her by the Chronicle for his own exculpation. It was stated previously that Macbeth in the first two acts is by no means the bloodthirsty tyrant of Holinshed and really stands far behind his wife in ambition. It is as if our poet, who plainly stands behind his hero, wished thereby to say, I am not capable of a father murder and would surely have put it off or not have accomplished it at all, if I had not been compelled by a woman's influence. Macbeth will go no further in the affair in spite of all favorable outward circumstances, but it is Lady Macbeth who forces the deed to completion. The final cause of every father hatred is rivalry in regard to the mother and so it was she, represented by Lady Macbeth, who in his phantasy would have urged the infantile Shakespeare to put his father out of the way. Here branches out another path for the sleep walking. We have so far spoken only of the father who comes at night to the child, but now Lady Macbeth walking in her sleep, seems also to represent Shakespeare's mother, who with the candle in her hand convinces herself that her darling child is sleeping soundly.[42]

[42] Going back into Shakespeare's own life gives further illumination and foundation for Lady Macbeth's behavior in the sleep walking scene. The reader may already have secretly thought that those little tendernesses on the part of ordinary parents hardly enter into consideration in the case of a thane's daughter. It may be said in answer to this that Shakespeare often, as in the presentation of ancient scenes, put without scruple the environment of

his own time in place of the historical setting. And according to the above he would be quite likely to utilize with Lady Macbeth recollections from the Stratford childhood.

It need not seem strange that I give a number of interpretations apparently so fundamentally different for one and the same thing. There is nothing on earth more complicated than psychic things, among which poetic creation belongs. Psychic phenomena are according to all experience never simply built up nor simply grounded but always brought together in manifold form. Whoever presses deeply into them discovers behind every psychic manifestation without exception an abundance of relationships and overdeterminations. We are accustomed in the natural sciences to simple motivation, on the one side cause, on the other effect. In the psychic life it is quite otherwise. Only a superficial psychology is satisfied with single causes. So manifold a chain of circumstances, those that lie near at hand and those more remotely connected, come into play in most, yes, apparently in all cases, that one scarcely has the right to assert that a psychic phenomenon has been completely explained. Dream analysis at once proves this. One can almost always rightfully take it for granted that several, indeed manifold interpretations are correct. It is best to think of a stratified structure. In the most superficial layer lies the most obvious explanation, in the second a somewhat more hidden one, and in yet deeper strata broader and more remote relationships and all have their part more or less in the manifested phenomenon. This latter is more or less well motivated.

We now turn back to Shakespeare and observe the great depression under which he labored just at the time when he created his greatest tragedies. Does it seem too presumptuous to conceive that one so shaken and dejected psychically should have slept badly and even possibly--we know so little of his life--walked in his sleep? The poet always hastened to repress[43] whatever personal revelations threatened to press through too plainly, as we know from many proofs. The poverty of motivation quite unusual with Shakespeare, just at the critical point of the sleep walking, seems to me to score for such a repression. We might perhaps say that the fact that the poet has introduced to such slight extent the wandering of Lady Macbeth, has given it so little connection with what went before, is due simply to this, that all sorts of most personal relationships were too much involved to allow him to be more explicit. See how Lady Macbeth comforted Macbeth directly after the frightful deed, the king and father murder:

"Consider it not so deeply. . . . . These deeds must not be thought After these ways; so, it will make us mad."

[43] Otto Rank in his book, "Das Inzest-Motiv in Dichtung und Sage," furnishes a beautiful and convincing example of such repression: It comes from a second drama based on a king's murder, "Julius Caesar." I quote from the author's words: "A heightened significance and at the same time an incontrovertible conclusiveness is given to our whole conception and interpretation of the son relationship of Brutus to Caesar by the circumstance that in the historical source, which Shakespeare evidently used and which he followed almost word for word, namely in Plutarch, it is shown that Caesar considered Brutus his illegitimate son. In this sense Caesar's outcry, which has become a catch-word, may be understood, which he may have uttered again and again when he saw Brutus pressing upon his body with drawn sword, 'And you too my son Brutus?' With Shakespeare the wounded Caesar merely calls out, 'Et tu Brute! Then fall, Caesar!   Shakespeare has set aside this son relationship of Brutus to Caesar, though doubtless known to the poet, in his working out of the traditional sources. Not only is there deep psychic ground for the modifications to which the poet subjects the historical and traditional circumstances and characters or the conceptions of his predecessor, but also for the omissions from the sources. These originate from the repressive tendency toward the exposure of impulses which work painfully and which are restrained as a result of the repression, and this was doubtless the case with Shakespeare in regard to his strongly affective father complex." Rank has in the same work demonstrated that this father complex runs through all of Shakespeare's dramatic work, from his first work, "Titus Andronicus," down to his very last tragedy. I cannot go into detail on this important point for my task here is merely to explain Lady Macbeth's sleep walking, but any one who is interested may find overwhelming abundance of evidence in Rank's book on incest (Chapter?). It is not only that I have introduced Shakespeare's strong father complex here to make comprehensible Lady Macbeth's sleep walking, but his own chief complex stood affectively in the foreground, and was worked out, at the same time, as Macbeth.

This must have referred to Shakespeare as much as to his hero. Moreover the writing and sealing of the letter at the beginning of the sleep walking described by the lady in waiting seems as if Lady Macbeth had a secret, a confession to make--in the name of the poet. I think also at the end, when the everlasting brooding over her deed drives her to suicide, she dies as a substitute for her intellectual creator, for his own self punishment.[44]

[44] I also recall that it is in fact she who expresses Duncan's character as father, "Had he not so resembled my father...."

There remain yet only one or two points to be touched upon and explained. No discussion is needed for the fact that an outspoken sadistic nature in Lady Macbeth leads her to walk in her sleep, indeed, disposes her to it. We can easily understand also that this breaks forth just at the moment when her husband sets out, that is, translated into the infantile, when Macbeth, or in the deeper layer her own father, dies. It is much more necessary to explain why immediately after the deed she has no scruples in staining the chamberlains with Duncan's blood and takes the affair so lightly, while later she is never rid of the fear of the blood and is always striving in vain to wash her hands clean. Here it must be again recalled that Lady Macbeth on the one hand represents the actual wife of Macbeth, on the other hand the poet himself and in two epochs of his life; Shakespeare first in his unrestrained striving and then when he is brought low, shaken in his very depths by the death of his father. Murder phantasies toward his father came to him as a boy and then as a youth at the beginning of puberty, and yet at neither time was he ill. The more mature man however, borne down more heavily by life, met by the actual death of his father, broke down under the weight of things. This explains in the last analysis the change in the attitude of Lady Macbeth.

I do not know how far the reader is willing to follow me. Yet one thing I believe I have proved, that also in Lady Macbeth's sleep walking the erotic is not wanting nor the regression into the infantile.

CONCLUSION

If now at the close of this book we bring together all our material, we may with certainty or with the highest probability speak of sleep walking and moon walking as follows:

1. Sleep walking under or without the influence of the moon represents a motor outbreak of the unconscious and serves, like the dream, the fulfilment

of secret, forbidden wishes, first of the present, behind which however infantile wishes regularly hide. Both prove themselves in all the cases analyzed more or less completely as of a sexual erotic nature.

2. Those wishes also which present themselves without disguise are mostly of the same nature. The leading wish may be claimed to be that the sleep walker, male or female, would climb into bed with the loved object as in childhood, which both the folk and the poet well know. The love object need not belong necessarily to the present, it can much more likely be one of earliest childhood.

3. Not infrequently the sleep walker identifies himself with the beloved person, sometimes even puts on his clothes, linen or outer garments, or imitates his manner to the life.

4. Sleep walking can also have an infantile prototype, when the child pretends to be asleep in order that it may be able, without fear of punishment, to experience all sorts of forbidden things, that is of a sexual nature, because it cannot be held accountable for that which it does "unconsciously, in its sleep." The same motive of not being held accountable actuates the adult sleep walker, who will satisfy his sexual desires, yet without incurring guilt in so doing. The same cause works also psychically, when sleep walking occurs mostly in the very deepest sleep, even if organic causes are likewise responsible for it.

5. The motor outbreak during sleep, which drives one from rest in bed and results in sleep walking and wandering under the light of the moon, may be referred to this, that all sleep walkers exhibit a heightened muscular irritability and muscle erotic, the endogenous excitement of which can compensate for the giving up of the rest in bed. In accordance with this these phenomena are especially frequent in the offspring of alcoholics, epileptics, sadists and hysterics with preponderating involvement of the motor apparatus.

6. Sleep walking and moon walking are in themselves as little symptoms of hysteria as of epilepsy. Yet they are found frequently in conjunction with the former.

7. The influence of the moon in this moon affectivity is very little known, especially in its psychic overdetermination. Yet there is little doubt that the moon's light is reminiscent of the light in the hand of a beloved parent, who every night came in loving solicitude to assure himself or herself of the child's sleep. Nothing so promptly wakes the sleep walker as the calling of his name, which accords with his being spoken to as a child by the parent. Fixed gazing upon the planet also has probably an erotic coloring like the staring of the hypnotizer to secure hypnosis. Other psychic overdeterminations appear merely to fit individual cases. It is possible finally that there actually exists a special power of attraction in the moon, which may expressly force the moon walker out of his bed and entice him to longer walks, but on this point we have no scientific hypotheses.

8. Furthermore it seems possible that sleep walking and moon walking may be permanently cured through Freud's psychoanalytic method.

I know very well that this explanation which I give here, offers only the first beginning of an understanding. It will be the task of a future, which we hope is not too far distant, to comprehend fully these puzzling phenomena.

###

www.ingramcontent.com/pod-product-compliance
Lightning Source LLC
Chambersburg PA
CBHW071046290526
45795CB00004B/1348